Having the world fam downside. Kidnapped i Israel during the Suez ~, Arab nations and French assassins. Fueled by intrigue and ever present danger, Michael created an imaginary world distanced from a typical adolescence. At age fifteen, he unintentionally crossed boundaries of decency with his father's trophy wife. The triangle shattered three lives. Abandoned to face life without his mentor, Michael befriended his destructive alter ego. Making an effort to reunite with his son, Leon invited sixteen-year old Michael on a global research trip including Austria, Afghanistan and Pakistan. And the two began an incredible journey that was destined to either destroy or mend what little remained of their relationship.

***

"Michael Uris's life story is worthy of one of his father's books. He reveals secrets that will astound you. Some of the account appears almost fictional, as if Michael's tale is an amalgam of imagination and reality. At its core, it is a love story. Though it encompasses one great romantic love, the central love is between father and son. Michael portrays the great love he had for his father and his father had for him, a love that was able to transcend some horrible truths. Leon Uris, to Michael, and to many of his readers, was larger than life, a great literary celebrity of his day. Michael shows how his father's very greatness impacted those who were closest to him. A fascinating read."

—Laurie Horowitz, Author, *The Family Fortune*

The Uris Trinity

The
Uris
Trinity

The father, the son and the trophy wife

A Memoir
Michael Cady Uris

RED SAFFRON PUBLICATIONS

Published by
Red Saffron Publications

Library of Congress Control Number: 2017934781

ISBN 978-0-9982700-3-6 Paperback
ISBN 978-0-9982700-4-3 Kindle Ebook
ISBN 978-0-9982700-2-9 Ebooks

Manufactured in the United States of America

First Edition October 2016
Second Edition February 2017

Book design by Stephanie Workman

www.michaelcadyuris.com

For Vicki Slotnick Paige

Light comes from darkness,
from quiet came the sound.
She freed me from my darkest vault,
and liberated my voice from silence.

Contents

Preface

Writing comes with the human race. We are genetically programmed to write. Writing chooses you. You don't choose writing. First of all you have to have some God-given talent. If you don't have that, you cannot develop it. You can develop some raw talent, but you can't make a smack-down wrestler out of an opera singer.

You also have to have powerful motivation. Something has to really be driving you to write. Pleasing our parents is the basis of all mankind and is usually the basis for that drive.

Understand, the worlds we live in are both real and imaginary. A writer takes from one world and gives to the other. If he cannot access the real world, he ventures further ahead in his own imagination. If he is trapped within his imagination, he can always find his way back to reality. Most people are trapped in their own subconscious minds because they are too embarrassed or ashamed of exposing who they really are and how they really feel. A writer sacrifices his own sanity to enter his subconscious to show to the world his innermost feelings.

We all have different boundaries for self-exposure. A writer has to unlock a series of doors. We go into the living room and we entertain and we show whom we are and we want to leave a good impression for our guests. Then we go into the den where we show a little more of ourselves to friends and family members. Then we have the bedroom where we show a lot of ourselves, but to relatively few people in a lifetime.

Then we have our private room where we win our Olympic medals and our arguments with our wives... idealistically speaking, everything in that room glows with brilliance and perfection.

Then, there is a locked room or vault we don't go into. The great writer sparingly immerses their conscious mind into the sludge and muck that permeates from one's deepest locked emotional vault. A place guarded by fear and repulsion. Inside that vault are your lies, your cheating, your greed, and a reflection of every evil thought you had since you were born. There you experience your own vicious reflection, one so hideous and vile that even seeing it for even a brief instant might cause you immense pain and a lifetime of remorse. And in the vault you cannot hide from your mirrored image, just as his sense of right and wrong forced Dorian Grey to view the canvas. Your vault is but a reflection of the dark side of your existence and even this side of you needs a place to survive.

Being honest with yourself is a very tough job. We are not only imperfect —we have done a lot of unmentionable things in our lives. It takes a lot of guts to write and most people cut that off before ever starting. They stop before that vault and say, 'I don't want to go in there.' A good writer never hesitates to enter that vault, for only in confronting our deepest fears can we expose what is really hidden in our hearts and soul. The factor that determines the true value of a great writer is how long they can tolerate residing in their deepest locked vault of feelings, desires, fears and emotions.

Leon and Michael Uris

Introduction

My father's favorite movie was *High Noon*. Every time it aired, he commanded my brother and me to sit down and watch it with him. Mark Jay, older and smarter than I, checked the TV listings ahead of time and would make up an elaborate story about having an important scouting event or a school project he needed to do at a classmate's house. My mother knew the excuses were fabrications, but she conspired in the deception.

That left me alone with Dad, not that I minded. I loved spending time with him even if I had to watch the same movie a hundred times.

The film opens on the day Sheriff Will Kane marries Amy Fowler. Kane resigns his position and the two are about to leave town to start a new life when Kane hears that a criminal he brought to justice is coming back to town on the noon train to seek his revenge. Kane could just leave; in fact, everyone tells him he should, but he stays to face the criminal and three others. The sheriff feels it's his duty to protect the town, even though no one in that town full of cowards will stand beside him. The sheriff must face the outlaws alone.

The film's suspense, intensity, and overwhelming odds never changed and eventually its message worked its way into my little brain. Winning the battle wasn't what mattered. What mattered was not backing down, not letting fear consume you or alter your intent. The act of facing your demons could make you invincible.

Sheriff Kane was an inspiration to my father. As Dad sat at the typewriter alone, he became the sheriff, and the outlaw gang who waited at the end of the dusty street for a showdown was the blank piece of paper. Like the sheriff, Dad never backed down. When my father wanted something, nothing could stop him. He planned. He assessed. He calculated. He would never make a move until he was assured that each character he'd imagined would arrive at the spot he desired. And then he would type the first word.

1

Exodus

Battle Cry, my father's first novel, came out the year I was born. It was a fictionalized account of my father's experience as a Marine during World War II. The book hit the bestseller list with a bang that would reverberate through our family for decades.

We—Mom, my sister Karen, my brother Mark Jay, Dad, and I—left our simple life in Larkspur near San Francisco, where Dad distributed newspapers to boys with paper routes. We were on our way to the glitzy environs of Hollywood.

I was not quite two years old when something happened that would set the tone of what was to be an unconventional childhood. I was kidnapped by our maid. It would be one thing if she had taken a shine to me or thought that my parents weren't paying me enough attention, but her reasons for running off with me were stranger than that. My father later told me his interpretation of what happened.

He said that the maid was consumed with jealousy and was worried that her husband was having an affair with my mother and wanted to run away with her. God forbid the woman could have just done it for the money like every other self-respecting kidnapper.

"The reasons she gave for your abduction were never clear," my father said.

Fortunately, I was recovered. Lee got the movie studio involved and for all I know that maid and her husband are lying in shallow graves outside Las Vegas. That's how things were then. If you worked for the studios and had any kind of profile, the studios used their own security forces to cover up any possible scandal.

I think being kidnapped as a child is closer to fiction than it is to real life. I recently looked up kidnappings in Wikipedia and found out two things, one more disturbing than the other. The first was that I am not listed (it being never reported to the police), and two, the majority of people who are kidnapped are subsequently murdered.

***

As to my life's story, some of it seems fictional, but what is fiction other than trying to convince the reader that what exists only in your imagination has its own reality. Whether or not these things actually happened (they did) somehow turned out to be beside the point. It's about getting the diamonds out of the mine, washing away the dirt, and finding what glitters among the debris. I trust in artistic vision as a means to an end. I am attempting to take you on a journey into the fifties, sixties and early seventies, into my life as the son of Leon Uris. In my father's books, he took you to Israel, to the Warsaw Ghetto, to Ireland, all over the world and through pivotal moments in history. His fiction worked on a visceral level, leaving his audience with both feelings and facts. Leon Uris' strength was in communicating heart to heart with a reader.

My father had an intellectual business savvy and a politically passionate side and my brother took after him. Mark was Dad's respectable self, the one with the ambitions and high ideals.

And then there was me.

As the second son, I reflected a different side of Dad. I became his jokester self, the jester, the trickster, and the one who rarely met a rule he wouldn't want to break. Mark stood under Dad's right arm, and I took his left. I was happy to be there. My brother and father were the two most important people in the world to me. If I had to stand in their shadows, then, as far as I was concerned, it was better than the glare of the sun.

Even in the shadows, it could get pretty warm, especially during Dad's celebrity moments when he and my mother Betty would have adult parties, or we were forced to tag along to some all-important event. And being the perfectly behaved children we were called upon to act as midget emissaries. I dutifully showed up, the little man all suited up with bowtie and formal shorts, ready to field questions from the guests, many of whom seemed to think that if they got close to the reflection of a celebrity, some of it would rub off on them:

'What is your dad working on next?'

'Do you think he'd read my screenplay?'

'Are you going to be a famous writer when you grow up?'

That was like asking me if I was going to be an esoteric philosopher. In fact, this is where I first developed claustrophobia and stammering, being surrounded by loud-mouthed tipsy giants who spewed cigarette smoke and intellectual jargon, all staring at me, waiting for my cute anecdotes to relieve the pressure of their ridiculous questions. Everyone enjoyed my nervous squirming and sweating, except for me. To them it was a social game, but for me these moments were traumatic. No matter how sincere my words, at times they couldn't help but mercilessly laugh at me. Thus, I learned the importance of having a famous father, that I was nothing more than a clown, a pathetic sideshow in the midst of his greatness. In striving to please my role model and mentor, I never gave in and suited up for the show with a smile on my face. With each new opportunity I gained a stronger foothold of understanding, and in time I stood with confidence as the center attraction, and watched the pathetic minions as they slurred disorderly words. I had an advantage that no one else did—I observed a highly intuitive writer every day, and I learned ways in the process of life that were both magical and well within my reach. Still, I knew my place and I would never set myself on the same pedestal as Leon Uris, but that hasn't kept me from putting pen to paper in an attempt to emulate a man I loved, even worshiped, at times.

My mother was a Marine Staff Sergeant. She sold war bonds during World War II. After several bouts of malaria, my father, a Marine combat radio operator in the Pacific Campaign, was sent stateside where he worked in the public relations department of the Marine Corps. My mother wrote home to her Danish Lutheran parents in Iowa to tell them that she had met the most marvelous man. His name was Leon Marcus Uris and he was going to conquer the world; he claimed he was going to be a world famous writer. He courted her with typed index cards sent from his desk to hers. She responded in kind. At first, she wasn't interested. My beautiful shiksa mother wanted someone taller. But my father's force of personality eventually won her over.

It wasn't until right before he asked her to marry him, that he dropped the Jew bomb. Up until then, she assumed he was Protestant, which wasn't hard since that's what he wanted everyone to think. It was much easier to be a gentile in the military in those days.

"He told me he was Jewish," my mother wrote home. "That's worse than being Catholic."

Mom's parents insisted that Leon wasn't the man for her. But his love eventually won over her heart, this she could not deny, and she wrote back to her parents to say that she was going to marry him no matter what they thought. He was charming, affectionate, intelligent, kind, and so full of energy he was almost bouncing off the walls. My mother was the small town farm girl. She left Iowa to join the Marines—not only for a sense of honor, but for the excitement of discovering a world that she'd been sheltered from, and what my father represented was far beyond anything she'd ever dreamed or imagined.

***

After we left Larkspur, my father worked on several screenplays, but he was blacklisted during the McCarthy era. At one point he was dragged into a meeting with a group of writers who were allegedly associated with the Communist Party. (My father was a registered member of the Communist Party before the war, and he was named after Leon Trotsky.) One of the writers was Ray Bradbury. After the government man gave his speech, my father got up, told the speaker what he thought of him, complete with every expletive he could think of, and marched out. Bradbury stood and followed him, along with a cadre of other writers. Years later, in the eighties, when my then wife was the costumer for a play of *The Martian Chronicles,* I had an opportunity to talk to Mr. Bradbury. In his version of the tale, he was the one who stood up and protested and it was my father and the other writers who followed him out. Not surprisingly, each of them had put themselves into the center of the story.

My father's second book *The Angry Hills* was your basic sophomore flop. He chose to write a spy novel about World War II and, apparently, he wasn't the only one with that idea, because there was a glut of these books on the market.

My father had, in a brief time, become acclimated to the good life and he knew he needed to do something big to resurrect his career.

"I want to write about Israel," Lee told Bennett Cerf, his publisher at Random House.

"That's a terrible idea. There has never been a successful novel written about contemporary Israel," Bennett said. My father had been tossing around another idea set in the world of prize fighting and Bennett suggested that Lee focus on that. "That's a winner. I like that idea," Bennett said.

Let's just say, my father could be a contrarian. He immediately mortgaged the house and flew straight to Israel.

As soon as Lee got there, he was sure he'd made the right decision. "I am sitting on the greatest book of all time," he wrote to my mother. "A miracle kept *Angry Hills* from ruining my career. I think I'm the best writer in the world, but I'm not going to depend on another miracle."

***

In 1957, Israel was not exactly the safest place in the world to be. My mother wanted my father to come back and write the book at home, but he was determined to stay on in Israel. He needed to work there if he wanted to create the masterpiece he envisioned. If Lee was going to suffer through the writing, he wanted the entire family to suffer as well. My poor mother didn't exactly see the necessity of this, but she took pity on him and before we knew it, the whole family was on its way to Israel so Dad could realize his dream.

We set up shop in a suburb of Tel Aviv in a small house on a hill. It had four rooms and a balcony. We even shipped the car.

In Israel, my sister went to a nearby American school and there we were, family life as usual. My mother wrote to her mother for necessary provisions: cookies, syrup, and chocolate. My mother's idea of adventure was living without peanut butter while my father's was to do things that would cause entire nations to hunt him down.

That year, there was at least one terror attack a month, from February to August, and we were evacuated in late October, due to the Suez crisis. With headlights and brake lights blacked out, we drove in the middle of the night to the American Air Force Base and were airlifted out of Israel just before dawn, along with many other families. We landed in Athens and then left for Italy. It was a rough ride, passengers vomiting, the cargo plane bouncing up and down. I had no idea what was really going on, but what I did understand was that the abundant love shared by our family was all that we could call our own.

We settled in Rome for a few weeks while we waited for my father to finish his side work as a war correspondent. Then he joined us and we sailed back to the United States via Barcelona to New York. From there we went to Philadelphia and then on to Iowa, then out to California, where my father finally planted his typewriter. Our lives had become the fuel that kept the fire burning, so my father could see his words come to life as he typed throughout the night. Metaphorically speaking, our family had experienced exactly what my father was seeking in order to write the masterpiece he envisioned. We'd become the Lost Tribe. And to my father, he finally fulfilled his promise to his ancestors by telling the story of Israel, and of the never-ending struggles of the proud Jewish people that had wandered for far too long without a homeland.

***

We moved back to Encino, to a house that had a separate office where my father wrote *Exodus*. And that's really where my consciousness begins, in that house, with my first test of bravery, at four years old. I was given the monumental task of bringing Dad an alcoholic drink, his afternoon pick-me-up.

My brother, sister and I were in the kitchen when my mother said, "Mark... it's time."

My brother stared at me. "Why don't you do it... or are you a coward?"

"Your brother is not a coward." My mother smiled at me. "You're a brave little man."

"Okay, I'll do it." I said in a firm voice. "Do what?"

"The devil needs a human sacrifice," my sister said.

"Your father needs a Martini." My mother rinsed out a glass.

"Oh that... but what about the demons?" I looked down at my feet.

"Bring your cap gun if you're afraid, coward," my brother said, laughing.

"Don't listen to Karen and Mark. They're just trying to scare you," Mom said.

I had been entrusted with a rare honor. Till then, I was nothing more than a mindless and basically worthless child. Doing this job that everyone else feared to do became my very first test of bravery, an honorable act. And if I died delivering the Martini, at least I would be remembered as someone brave and not for being a coward.

My brother and sister had told me that the only reason Dad had an office was to keep his demons contained in one place. He was working on the finishing touches of his novel. My siblings swore that Dad's demons would be on the loose and running rampant and out of control in his office. They told me that Dad made a deal with the devil to allow the forces of evil to enter his workplace and help him write his novels. It was nearly impossible to guess exactly what kind of a mood my father would be in. And around the same time, every late afternoon, one family member had to be sacrificed. Someone had to venture into the fires of hell to face the wrath of pure evil and deliver a neatly prepared, filled to the very brim, stirred and never shaken, vodka Martini with a toothpick skewering two green olives and a pickled onion.

Even though my brother and sister never seemed too distressed after they returned from delivering the sacred vessel of elixir, I imagined them being chased around the office by flying demons and nearly perishing under the stress. The horrible stories they recalled inspired me with terror. Ever since I was old enough to understand words, my siblings told tales of blood red monsters flying around inside Dad's office, and Dad himself was transformed into the most powerful demon, ready to torture and murder the next person to walk into his office unannounced.

I had been in my father's office plenty of times and had never seen any such demons, but my father wasn't feverishly typing away at the time. What was I supposed to believe, my own eyes or the scary warnings from my siblings? It was common knowledge around our household that if Dad was sitting behind the typewriter working on a book, we should stay away, hide if we must. Loud noises were out. No slamming doors or yelling. We could only disturb him if the house was on fire.

For nearly the first four years of my life, my mother, brother and sister had been nice to me. They happily patronized me and made me feel loved and cherished. They stood by my side in the face of any and all adversity. Was my entire life a lie? Had my family been cleverly preparing me all those four years for becoming nothing more than a human sacrifice?

In our Encino home, Dad's office across the driveway seemed to be miles away from the main house. The journey was the longest hundred footsteps in the world. Mom cheerfully loaded up the traditional wide rimmed martini glass to the brim. I knew her pleasant demeanor was only a ruse to conceal the fact that she was willing to sacrifice her youngest child in order to escape a terrible fate herself. As a precaution, I took my brother's advice and slipped a loaded cap gun into my back pocket in case I had to shoot down any flying demons.

What an impossible task. What if I tripped and spilled the entire contents of the glass? Would I be cast out into the world, have to change my name and live a life of abandonment and hardship? If I spilled even a few drops and returned to get a refill, would my Mom scold me and forbid me from ever watching the *"Mickey Mouse Club House"* again? And if Dad discovered even one drop missing, would he lash out in an uncontrollable rage and tell Santa I didn't deserve any gifts for the rest of my life and then unleash the hidden demons in his office to devour me? Whatever my fate, I decided to become the family hero. I would not spill a single drop. I'd face my dad, no matter what mood he was in, no matter how red his eyes were or how harsh his language. And then I'd return to my mom and siblings, no longer a coward, but as someone they could trust to do their dirty work.

This was the first time in my life that I could remember sweating profusely. I was a nervous wreck, but dared not lose my grip. Onward I walked, slower than our pet turtle, step-by-step, holding the glass at eye level, and allowing for every form of fear and anxiety to enter my mind. Still, I made that courageous journey without spilling one drop.

With multitasking skills extraordinaire, I held the doorknob between my shoulder and ear, and turned it. Ever so cautiously, I entered my father's office. Much to my relief, there were no flying demons and Dad didn't look angry or satanic in the least. Bravely, I handed him one vodka Martini filled to the very brim. Dad graciously took the drink. After taking a first sip, he gave me a big smile and a kiss on the cheek. He then asked me to make another voyage to the kitchen for a bowl of cauliflower, celery and carrot sticks.

I returned a few minutes later and Dad let me sit on his knee while he sipped his drink. We shared the bowl of vegetables while he continued to make some finishing touches on the daily typing. Before long, the bowl was empty and the Martini had disappeared. Dad had even found the inspiration to venture onto a new page.

I sat in amazement, sharing my time between watching the enthusiastic glow of my father's smile and the words forming on the page. With each carefully regimented movement of his fingers on the keyboard, a new word was created. Eventually, the words merged with others and sentences were formed. An entire page appeared, filled with words where once there were none. Then, without hesitation, Dad loaded another blank piece of paper into the machine.

Even though I was sitting on his knee, an invader in his realm, Dad made every effort to make me feel welcome, yet it was apparent that the lion's share of his concentration was elsewhere. As each new word was stamped upon the paper, I continued to watch the very subtle glimmer in his eyes and radiance of his smile. The relationship he had with his newly formed creation was one of both wonder and surprise.

So this is what my dad did for a living. And the wild stories of flying demons in his office became clear to me. For Dad to face a blank piece of paper was his greatest fear, the showdown at *High Noon*, and once a single letter was typed, his flying demons were kept at bay.

And when the day's work was done and he typed the last word, he turned his complete attention toward me and smiled. I cannot recall him ever being so elated and proud. And the feeling of his accomplishment overwhelmed me as well. It was then I noticed that a single tear escaped from his eye.

"Why are you crying?" I asked.

"If I get all the words on a page just right, my heart lets me know the words are in perfect order by releasing one single tear."

"Because you are sad?" I asked.

"Because my heart is pleased. Though sometimes the words I type are sad. They have to be to tell the story."

"Like when someone tells a sad story about a person or a pet dying?"

"Yes, but there are also tears of joy. When your heart is touched or something moves you," Dad said.

"I guess your heart is pretty busy."

"My heart does most of the work. Without understanding the heart, I could not write at all," Dad confessed.

"Why do you write?" I asked.

"To offer my perspective. To not only relate historical events throughout history, as they actually happened, but also to show the feelings that motivated those events. What is in a man's heart has more meaning than the wealth he can carry in his arms. I offer the feelings in my heart, through a simple display of words to others so that they can awaken those same feelings in their own hearts."

"If your feelings are hidden in your heart, how do you find them?"

Dad took a few moments to find the proper answer. "With the light of discernment."

"Dis... what?"

"I allow the most precious feelings and mysteries of the world to be understood."

"Dad, how do you know these mysteries can be understood?"

"When the words come from my heart and touch the heart of the reader, both the mysteries and feelings are passed on, and my job is done."

"And the reader's heart releases a tear."

Dad kissed me on the forehead. "You do understand."

"What do I understand?"

"As much as you need to right now. In time I will teach you as much as you wish to know." Dad smiled. "The subtle mysteries of life and eternity wait for us all."

"Can the mysteries wait till tomorrow? Mom is making spaghetti for dinner." Still, something remained unclear to me. "Do you believe in God?"

"I believe there is a power greater than any one man or woman, a power greater than the entire universe. A force greater than nature that created and watches over us all."

"Where did you learn that?"

"My ancestors believed in God."

"What is an ancestor?"

"My parents and my father's parents and their parents before them, going back thousands of years. My ancestors are also your ancestors."

"I guess we all came from somewhere." I scratched my head. "Mom said you don't write about real people. Is your story about Israel make-believe?"

"My story about Israel is mostly real but some of the people are make-believe." Although Dad realized I was too young to fully understand, I think talking to me was a way to sort out his own feelings.

"This is what my father once told me," he said. "Our ancestors were responsible for protecting the people of Israel and their homeland. Our ancestors even died for freedom. Israel represents our right to exist and to be free. Everyone sees the world from a different angle. I choose storytelling and make-believe characters to best tell the stories of our ancestors." Dad stared at me, then smiled as he added, "Maybe by the time you grow up, you will understand."

"Mark Jay said you test him to make sure he is listening to you. A lot of your words are confusing so I hope you don't test me. Mark Jay said his teacher thinks you are someone special."

"Son, we are all special." Dad chuckled. "When I was your age my father used to call me his little Metatron."

"Sounds like a robot."

"He's an important angel in Judaism."

"What does the angel do?"

"He's a guardian angel. He allows hearts to feel and souls to understand the hidden mysteries of life. He knows that everyone can be good, if they choose to be." Dad glanced at the pages on the desk. "To do good things in life we must first be happy with ourselves," he added.

"Are you happy?" I asked.

Dad smiled. "If I am sad, I think about you being happy and then I am happy again. Never forget, when you are happy, it gives me a reason to be happy."

"I'll remember that."

In a robot voice, Dad asked, "Would-you-like-to-play-catch-before-dinner?"

I jumped off his knee onto the floor. "I'm glad that you're not an evil demon."

"Would you love me any less if I was?"

"Nothing could make me love you less." I ran toward the door. "If I became evil, would you love me less?"

"I have faith in you, Son. Even if the world turns against you, eventually you will make the right decisions and do what is good."

"I feel the same about you."

2

Fuckin' French Assassin

"Fuck you, Dad!" I screamed. I slammed down the phone receiver. It was February 19, 1967, the day I turned fourteen.

My brother and I lived with our mother in California and my father lived in Colorado. We were all suffering due to my parent's separation and pending divorce.

Dad's intentions were good; he wanted to wish me a happy birthday, but we ended up in a fight and I hung up on him. It was easier for both of us to cool off for a few minutes before continuing the conversation. My father called back and we resumed our talk as though nothing was out of the ordinary.

Just one week before, my brother and I received this letter from Lee:

Dear Mark and Mike,

When I left home twenty five years ago to join the Marines, there existed a very poor relationship between my father and me and my unhappiness was one of the causes of my running away.

Since that time my father has demanded that I write and even though I resented this forced correspondence I have been faithful in my letters because my father has certain rights that I will honor out of a sense of duty and responsibility.

We do not have such a relationship. I was certain that we were closer than most fathers and sons. It is hard enough living apart but you are now bringing about a complete breakdown in communications where I am shut out of your life and aspirations.

But even though you don't have the sense of honor or duty or responsibility to do what's right I would think that out of common decency you would behave better toward the person who is feeding and clothing you.

I hoped we would stay in close contact, because you love me and want and need to continue and enjoy our relationship. I deplore your behavior and think you both are lazy ingrates.

But I am making no demands on you nor will this subject come up again. Just bear in mind that everything you do or don't do in this world will come back to you some day and you'll be paid good for good and bad for bad. You are setting the stage for a future of indifference between us, and a chance to become total strangers. I think you'll regret this sorely. And don't believe for a minute that I won't write you off the way you are writing me off. You are going to be treated by me exactly the same way you are treating me. Call me on your birthday if it's not too much trouble.

As ever, Dad

My mother responded:

Dear Lee,

Although they rarely if ever admit it, the boys miss you all the time. They know you love them and I know you love them. Their love for you is deep and real. I have criticized your fathering because of your lack of time and attention for them but I know you have love for them. I pray it is love for them for who they are, unconditional love for them as individuals, and not love for them because of what they do for you. What means little to the boys is that you are a humanitarian and a famous celebrity, what means everything to them is that you are a good father. And always be that man that means everything to them, because in your heart I know their love means everything to you.

Love, Betty

By the time Mom sent off her letter, Dad had called to apologize about his. He was frustrated and upset about our family breaking up and he said he didn't mean what he had written. He hoped we understood that because of the divorce, there would probably be times like this ahead.

My father lived in two worlds, that of reality and that of imagination. His fictional and glamorized version of the truth was no less real than daily life. When real life became too boring, he dove into a world of illusion. When his imagination suffered from claustrophobic conditions, he jumped back into reality. What he forgot to tell any of his loved ones, was which Leon Uris we were dealing with at any given moment.

Dad led an extremely exciting life, far more interesting than any work of fiction. Through his craft, he transformed emotionless facts into explosive recreations with depth and feeling. His storytelling remained fact based. He was inspired by history.

At a very early age, I was intrigued by my father's thought process. I watched him create something out of nothing, and witnessed him influence the greatest minds of our time. I considered my father divinely inspired and thought that there was no man who came close to making the contributions he did.

***

In 1967, my brother and I lived in Malibu, and my father showed up in tinsel town to do technical work on a screenplay for his novel *Mila 18*, a very passionate story of Poland's Warsaw Ghetto uprising during the Nazi occupation of World War II.

Situated in a lofty tenth floor corner suite of a Sunset Strip hotel, Dad was casting stars to play the book's leading characters. It was early evening as my brother and I, aged sixteen and fourteen, entered Dad's suite. One of the potential stars was just leaving. The up and coming *Raw Hide* television star had a couple of spaghetti westerns to his name. Tall, with shoulders large enough to fill the doorway, he was soft spoken and polite. The man was none other than the future mayor of Carmel, Clint Eastwood. He was there to be interviewed for the lead character. Unfortunately for both Lee and Clint the movie was never made.

As always, Lee maintained his integrity and insisted on respect for the content of his books. In consequence, he had trouble finding producers to back his movie ventures with funds acquired from legitimate sources. People would give him money to produce his work, but when he checked out some of the backers, they weren't Lee's idea of legit. Whether it was the Mob or a Republican politician Lee couldn't stomach, he wouldn't take what he called "funny money."

He wrote scripts for most of his novels, and only *Battle Cry* was made without my father backing out of the deal, or being fired by the director. Otto Preminger fired Dad from *Exodus* and Alfred Hitchcock fired him from *Topaz*, both directors claimed, "Uris did not understand the story."

Both movies were critically destroyed. The family watched Exodus with Lee at the studio's screening room and one of the worst experiences of my young life was enduring Lee heckling the movie from the beginning to end. We lost our appetites. We were supposed to go to dinner, but we drove straight home and had TV dinners in front of the *Ed Sullivan Show*.

***

That evening back in 1967, Mark Jay and I entered Lee's hotel suite. After saying our hellos, we all walked over to the window and watched the colorful evening lights emanating from the prominently displayed billboards and nightspots along the famous Sunset Strip. Afterward, we boys sat on a couch. I focused my attention on strategically eating every grape in the coffee table fruit display while Mark Jay's twitching fingers thumbed through the latest issue of *Playboy Magazine*.

Dad became increasingly nervous and paced back and forth across the length of the thirty-foot suite. It was obvious that he was searching for exactly the right dialogue to present us with, a tedious exercise my brother and I were familiar with. After pouring himself a stiff drink, Dad threw it down the hatch and poured another.

Eventually, he grabbed two eight by ten glossy black and white photographs and handed one to each of us. It was a headshot of a well-dressed gentleman wearing a suit. Mark Jay and I focused all our attention on the picture and waited for our father to speak.

My father's novel *Topaz* was published that year. *Topaz* is a fictionalized account of how French Intelligence turned a blind eye and allowed Soviet nuclear missiles to be sent to Cuba during the Cuban Missile Crisis in 1962, six days that culminated in a nuclear showdown between President Kennedy and Soviet Premier Khrushchev.

In almost a panic, Dad exclaimed, "He's an assassin hired by—I don't know who—probably French Intelligence—or should I say those fucking French—are just a little agitated that I exposed their pact with the Soviets in *Topaz*. Those bastards are sending this coward to murder me!"

Mark corrected, "Didn't you mean to say, those cowards are sending this bastard. Doesn't that make more sense?"

Dad downed his second drink and poured another.

I added, "French is a weird language."

"Yeah," my brother added. "They do embarrassing stuff, like surrendering and showing tits on television."

Dad drank the drink in one swallow.

Naturally, my brother and I started to smirk and giggle. This was not the first time our father came up with such a crazy sounding revelation.

Earlier that same year, during the Six Day War (June 1967), the Israeli army captured East Jerusalem from Jordanian control. When the Israeli troops stormed one of the highest-ranking Arab strongholds within the ancient city, they discovered the 'Arab Nation's least popular people in the world list.' It listed top benefactors, statesmen, and general contributors to the State of Israel. Topping the list were the two Rothschild brothers, but third on the list was Leon Uris. Not only had Lee written *Exodus* and *Mila 18*, he had also given numerous speeches at fundraisers to benefit the growth of Israel and bring acceptance and support for the Jewish struggle in the Middle East and throughout the world.

The Israeli Government informed Dad about his appearance on the list. Dad found it necessary to inform my brother and me that he might not have long to live. Lee had no idea of the exact meaning of his placement on the list, but he was not going to take any chances when it came to the overall safety of his family. Lee wasn't trying to frighten or panic us. He just wanted us to be more conscious of our surroundings and the people we dealt with.

Though my brother remained silently cautious, I started to collect firearms and various instruments of war. I carried concealed weapons most wherever I went. Back in those days anyone could buy a firearm or gunpowder at any drug or hardware store. A junior high school buddy of mine taught me how to make bombs. I never used guns to hunt; I only kept weapons for self-defense, just in case a small invading army came to our house. Death threats on my father's life came in the mail on a regular basis. He wrote about the vilest acts of humanity and was not afraid to point his finger at the responsible parties, and they were not afraid to point right back. While other kids at school stressed over a pimple or whom to invite to their birthday parties, I calmly wondered if the Syrians were going to torture me, then kill me, or just surprise me with a high velocity sniper bullet.

My mother became concerned when she discovered a new weapon hidden in my room every couple of days. She sent me to a psychiatrist who I saw on a weekly basis. Looking back, I do not regret my actions, and in spite of her concern I continued to arm myself whenever I ventured out into the vast wasteland of the real world.

Sometimes, my brother and I could barely figure out if our father was telling us the truth, or just using us as sounding boards for his imagination. A great deal of our lives with Dad was borderline theater of the absurd.

***

"I wish it was a joke!" Dad feverishly pointed to the reverse side of the photo. The back of the photo listed the man's name, height, weight, other unique physical characteristics, and last known address. The list included the phone numbers for the FBI (and Interpol) field offices in Los Angeles, Denver, and Grand Junction. As I pretended to study the information, Dad stole the *Playboy* from my brother and became mesmerized by some blossoming hussy.

Dad exclaimed, "This doesn't seem real."

"You're right," said Mark Jay. "The blond had a boob-job."

Smiling with gritted teeth, Dad said, "I was referring to the guy in the photo."

I looked at the photo. "This guy doesn't have big tits, and he isn't blond."

Dad lifted his hand as though he was going to backhand me across the face. He then smiled and lowered his hand. "Just study the information on the back of the photo."

We studied the photo and related data. It was amazing we did not burst out laughing. Every time Lee would focus all this attention on a picture of a naked lady in the magazine, Mark and I would make clown faces and scratch our armpits like apes. This went on for a few minutes. Finally, when Lee put down the *Playboy*, my brother dropped the photo and scrambled for the magazine.

The photograph of the alleged assassin and related information strangely captivated my attention. This new revelation added such importance to my existence that I could hardly contain myself. My father's legitimate concern for our safety added prominence and power to my already abundant paranoia.

While gazing at the photograph, my imagination transported me into numerous scenarios, each one more incredible than the last. I imagined spies entering the room and trying to murder us... or possibly a team of assassins rappelling off the side of the building and targeting us through a window... or a sniper on one of the nearby buildings... or a helicopter hovering just outside the window and taking us out with a .50 caliber machinegun... or housekeeping would show up to turn down the bed while we were out to dinner and she'd poison Dad's mouthwash. And those were just the thoughts that came to me in the first few minutes. The rest of my ruminations stood waiting in a line that went around the block. There was no limit to my imagination, or my paranoia. My father's books were the source of my survival in an imaginary world of wars, spies, and international intrigue.

It was clearly understood in our family that Lee was one of the great voices for the human struggle. Even though he maintained ridiculously high levels of self-importance, he did actually care, not only about the people in his life, but for all of humanity. It tore him apart to know that some of his words helped some, while those same words harmed others. He had a message to deliver and if someone needed to threaten violence to shut him down, he was willing to accept that. He took responsibility for his actions and taught us to do the same. Sacrifices had to be made for the greater good.

My brother pointed at the picture of the assassin. "Dad, he looks just like the *77 Sunset Strip* television star, Efrem Zimbalist Jr."

"Yeah," I added. "If they ever make a movie about Dad, they can hire Efrem to play the assassin."

Lee sat down in a chair facing the couch, leaned back and closed his eyes. My brother aggressively thumbed through the *Playboy*, and I polished off the last grape. A couple of minutes later, Dad took the *Playboy* from my brother and gently tossed it just out of reach.

"Boys, if anything should ever happen to me, if I die for any reason, I want you to immediately order an autopsy and then kill that fucking French assassin." Dad pointed at the photograph.

"You die. Get an autopsy. Then kill the fucking guy. Okay. Got it," I said. "Now can we go to that deli down the street?"

"And don't forget to call the FBI!" Dad pointed at me in all sincerity.

"When do we call the FBI?"

"As soon as you suspect anything!"

I looked out the window. "Is the FBI watching us right now?"

"Who knows?" Dad answered, "Maybe they're tracking the whereabouts of the assassin."

"Doesn't sound like they are doing anything other than scaring us. Maybe we should go after this guy ourselves," I said.

Dad smiled.

Mark Jay chuckled. "Any more brilliant ideas?"

"We can use Dad as a decoy to flush out the guy." I thought for a moment. "We'll hire a group of actors... and then have a makeup specialist disguise all of them to look like Dad... and then the fucking assassin will get confused and..."

"Can we go to dinner?" Mark Jay asked.

"I think we should call the FBI right now," I said.

Frustrated, Dad's eyes turned red. "Are you still seeing that psychiatrist?"

"Are you angry with me?"

"Son, sometimes I don't know if you're serious or just joking. Either case, this is really no laughing matter, nor is it a reason to do something foolish." Dad took a couple of deep breaths and scratched his forehead. Then he looked at me and said, "Your mother is pretty upset, and worried about you."

"Don't worry about Mike. He's not the type to hunt down an assassin," my brother said.

"If something happened to Dad what would you do?" I asked my brother.

"I'll worry about it when the time comes," Mark Jay said.

"When the time comes it will be too late." I stared at my brother.

Dad faced Mark Jay. "Your little brother isn't the type to wait for the phone to ring. And when he says he thinks it's a good idea to go after the French assassin, don't think for a moment he's not serious. Just look at him. Something's going on in that head."

"He looks stupid," Mark Jay said.

"Don't call your little brother stupid."

"I said he looks stupid, not that he is stupid," my brother corrected.

"I'm hungry." I said. "Either we go to dinner or we call the FBI."

"And tell them what?" Dad was barking now. He was getting aggravated with me.

"Do I have to do your thinking for you?" I said.

Mark Jay laughed. Dad gave me one of those 'this had better be good' looks.

"See if they even care," I said. "Speak to the guy in charge of the investigation. Dad, do you even know his fucking name? I don't care, ask them what the hell is going on and demand a daily update. Let them know you are watching their moves as well. Open up a fucking line of communication... you know Dad... like the one you demand that Mark and I have with you... tell those gum shoe dicks at the bureau anything you want... tell them that you're going to a Jewish deli for dinner and you're worried about being mobbed by Holocaust survivors."

"Mike, promise me you won't do anything foolish."

Mark laughed.

I looked at my father with sincerity in my eyes. "I'm not trying to be foolish." I walked over and gave my dad a hug. "You mean a lot to me and I don't want you getting hurt, or dead. My psychiatrist said if you have a good reason, it is smart to be somewhat paranoid. If having a fucking French assassin trying to kill my dad is not a good enough reason to be seriously paranoid, then what is?"

Lee just stared at me. I had no idea what was going through his head.

I pointed directly at Lee, just like he had always pointed at us boys. "You taught us not to take chances, and when we turn our backs, you take those chances anyway. To protect the ones you love, there is no question about sacrificing your life. Now it's my turn to show you how it's done. So, don't even try to stop me. I am going to do it anyway. You can't stop an assassin with words. I'm going to get him before he has you in his crosshairs."

Dad smiled and nodded in respect. "I think it's time to get some dinner."

Canters on Fairfax is one of those tacky old world Jewish delis, with the art deco low-backed booths made out of laminated plastic, and a brightly lit warm and friendly fifties style atmosphere. Every Jew within fifty miles is magnetically drawn to Canter's schmaltzy charm.

The three of us chose a booth somewhere near the middle of the room in hopes of being able to grab the attention of one of Canter's lovely and sweet, yet nearly blind and hard of hearing, geriatric waitresses.

After our waitress brought our dinner the three of us couldn't have been happier. While eating matzo ball soup and Swiss cheese on rye sandwiches with our father by our side, we tried our best to relax. Although we didn't talk about assassination attempts or French Intelligence during dinner, my brother and I were faced with sudden responsibility. We would have to grow a foot taller before the morning. And there would never be any chance of reverting back to the age of innocence. From now on we would have to be watchful of our surroundings, and be constantly aware of the dangers that waited for us.

Dad had given us our wake-up call. We were supposed to grow up and pay attention. Arising from the ashes of a broken family, the three male members of the Uris family would have to remain united and form a lifelong bond. That bond had little to do with foiling international assassination plots; it meant we would always be there for each other.

I remember a recording of Segovia playing in the background. The classical guitarist played a beautiful arrangement from his heart. Although surrealistic in nature, considering the imminent danger involved, these were perfect moments in time.

Near the end of the meal I said, "The reason why I started collecting weapons is because I want to be prepared. I didn't tell Mom what they were for. Dad, does she know about all of this, the French and the Arab Nations?"

"I've been meaning to tell her..."

My brother cut Lee off. "It's okay, Dad. She doesn't need to know about the French and the Arabs. She already knows people are angry with you. No reason to piss her off more than she already is."

"Your mother has enough to worry about, with the divorce and starting a new life."

"That's why I didn't tell her the truth. I let her think I'm just a suicidal nutcase." I took a final bite of my sandwich.

"You are a fucking nutcase," my brother said.

I gave him a stern expression and then flipped him the bird.

Mark Jay made silly faces at me and scratched under his arms like a monkey.

"All of us are nutcases." Dad turned to Mark. "Did you think for just one minute that maybe your brother is trying to look out for your safety, and your mother's? Maybe it's time we all start appreciating each other, before it's too late."

"I'm not trying to be funny," Mark replied. "Dad, you told us there were several Arab nations that wish you were dead. Well, that sucks. I'll go all Chuck Norris on them if you want me to. Now you tell us a French assassin is targeting you. I'm not happy about it. I want to know who is in charge of your case at the bureau. I want updates and answers. And that French fry had better take a good long look in the mirror—and say au revoir. If my brother goes after that Frenchman, he's not going to be alone. I'm going to be right there by his side."

3

The Triangle

Lee met Margery Edwards in Aspen around 1966. At the time he was still living with my mother. No longer able to tolerate his infidelity, my mother packed up the station wagon. Along with Mark Jay, the family dog, and me, we drove to Iowa to spend the summer with Betty's Danish parents. When Mom told us to pack up and get in the car, I didn't know what it all meant. It was a two-day drive, but my mother drove straight through and she didn't say much.

I remember listening to a song on the radio—*I'm coming to take you away ha ha ho ho, to the funny farm where life is beautiful all day long.* My mother reached over and turned it off.

"Enough of that," she said.

When we reached my grandparent's house, my mother broke out in tears and bolted from the car into her mother's waiting arms.

I was thirteen, and it was only then that I realized my family life, as I had known it, was over. I tried to convince myself that it was just a cooling off period, that eventually we'd all go back to Aspen together, but that was not to be.

My father filed for divorce a week later. The notice appeared in the *Los Angeles Times.*

Seeks Divorce

● Author **Leon Uris** has filed suit for divorce from **Mrs. Betty K. Uris**, it was disclosed. The action was filed June 14 in Aspen, Colo., and charged mental cruelty. Uris is the author of "Exodus" and "Armageddon."

The divorce, filed on the grounds of mental cruelty, took two years. My father's expensive team of trial lawyers pulverized my mother's well-intentioned Iowa brother-in-law lawyer into cornmeal. In God's eye my uncle Bill won a decisive moral victory.

Mark Jay believed Margery was the cause of my parents' break up and so he had little to do with her. He thought Margery was a gold digger, and he always took Mom's side. If Margery was the cause of the break-up, I never blamed her. When I looked at her, I saw the perfect woman. She was a rare beauty with a classic East Coast style. When she walked, all eyes were on her. It was as if she was floating through the room. She had come straight out of a *Playboy Magazine*, and I couldn't blame my father for falling in love with her. Dad wanted to move on, and Margery was the woman he chose.

Dad's infatuation with Margery sometimes clouded his judgment. He jumped into his new marriage mere months after his divorce was finalized and didn't even ask for a prenuptial agreement. Unlike my brother, I didn't believe Margery was in it for the money. She could easily find that on her own. What she wanted was Dad's affection. He had a big personality, and she loved the side of him that he offered her in the early days. She couldn't see the monster behind the door. Again, Dad had created a fictionalized character: he was the great humanitarian, God's gift to literature, the wealthy, worldly man. What lurked behind the facade were his impatience, his unresolved frustrations, and an ego the size of Manhattan.

Lee could be eating breakfast and reading his mail and suddenly, he'd start to stare at someone at the table. "I'm disgusted with you," he'd say. Then, he'd run his hand over his head and squeeze his chin. "You're not a happy person. You're dragging me down. How come I have to do your thinking for you? Don't you have a mind of your own? I'm the person who puts the food on the table, who gives you clothes and a house. I spend all my time making a good life for you and what do I get in return—nothing. I get pain, resentment, and constant rejection. I'm going to my office." Off he would go, leaving whoever was so unfortunate to be caught in his headlights devastated. Later, you might get buzzed from his office. "Wanna play tennis?" And the angry man was gone. Just like that. But he'd be back. The angry man was the one who was subjected to one adversary after another, who handled the death threats, the lawsuits, and the complicated legal contracts. Whether in personal or public life, I don't remember my father ever conceding to anything.

Margery was Lee's opposite, innocent and sweet. Daily life with my father eventually unraveled her like delicate tapestry exposed to a hurricane.

Having been around Dad all my life, I took his behavior for granted. Conflict was our way of life. Without a challenge from an adversary, how could the hero ever rise to the call? To separate Dad's inflated image from what a real person should be often confused me. I was eight or nine when I realized that my father lived mainly in his imagination and the person he presented wasn't real. But by then I was far from being able to distinguish what was real and what wasn't. Eventually, I would learn to exist in my own right, not solely as the son of Leon Uris, but that would take some time. My brother was smarter than I was. He somehow found his identity earlier and without such trauma.

My father had three very distinct personas: one was public, charming and very respectable, the second face was strategic, cunning and fact-based to a fault. My brother reflected both of these personas. Then there was the wild, abundantly creative, carefree, and devilish man that very few people knew. It was this alter ego that attracted me. I believed this to be the best of Leon Uris, the side that enjoyed every sip of life as if it were priceless wine. And I, the sponge, soaked it up.

***

Dad and Margery's need for a buffer to make their relationship work increased. Sometimes hired help fulfilled the role, but these people only saw the public side of Leon and Margery. I was the perfect buffer, because where my father really shone with Margery was when he was the iconoclast, the man I thought was the real Leon Uris. With me around, Dad never had to put on a mask. He raised me to reflect the prankster in him, all that was unruly and nonconformist.

Brought up in the Northeast, Margery harbored many old world inhibitions, many of which complemented my father's public personality. Unsuspecting my father's grand design, I became an irreplaceable character in his newest play, the bridge between Margery and my father's alter ego.

Lee was a busy man and left Margery to do as she pleased. She shopped or added personal touches to the house. Even though we had a daily maid Monday through Friday, Margery arranged all the meals and took care of social obligations. Dad would sit at the breakfast table and write a list of things each of us should do and hand them out. For me, it was taking care of the dogs, getting the mail, shining shoes—things like that. For Margery, it was planning parties, choosing gifts, cooking, and household shopping. We took care of my father, both as a man and a corporate entity. We never had a schedule. Everything floated along with Dad's needs. I became the third wheel who helped them through their busy days.

***

Like all the characters in Lee's life, Margery had her scripted role. He didn't want her to go out into town unescorted where jetsetters and the bar scene flourished. His jealousy isolated her from the world, and ironically he stuck her with harmless me.

Our relationship began as nothing more than fun and a common fight against boredom. The first time Margery caught me off guard, my punishment was a good tickling. From there we chased each other around like school kids, playing games, adding laughs and timeouts to catch our breaths. In public we had snowball fights, skied and played tennis. Although innocent in nature, in private our encounters tested the boundaries of respectability that were never clearly defined.

Lee often came out of his office to grab a snack when Margery and I were in the living room. I'd be reading poetry—Rumi or Kabir—with Margery's head in my lap. Dad would give me a friendly touch on the shoulder as he passed us.

When I recited poetry to Margery, I didn't stammer, and I had always stammered, especially when I read. Even if I read a short newspaper article aloud, my words would come out scrambled. It embarrassed me, but it may have embarrassed my father more. I found the best way to deal with it was not to put myself into a position where it would happen. Reading to Margery changed all that. It allowed me to open up and my father was pleased.

"I'm glad you two are getting along so well," he said at dinner. "Margery, you have come to life. Mike, I appreciate you spending so much time with Margery."

Margery took black and white photos around Aspen, and I often went with her. She had a room setup downstairs where she made jewelry, and she taught me how to solder silver. We spent a couple hours a week down there making rings, cuff links, and pendants.

***

Paying close attention to detail, she was my personal fashion consultant. She wanted to make sure every hair was in place and that my clothing matched and fit to perfection. She liked to help me choose my clothes. Sharp and respectable were Dad's words. That was how he wanted me to look, and he was big on me being well groomed. I was only a teenager; till then I didn't use deodorant, and I rarely brushed my hair. It was Margery who got me to pull myself together, complete with the right shampoos and manly scents. I might have been a slob, but I was willing to change for Margery.

When we finished with the mandatory lists that Lee gave us, it was time to do our own thing. We were castaways—often laughing at my mature reformation. That usually led to one of us pinning the other down, and then relentless tickling began. Sometimes, it would turn into a wrestling match that ended in a hug. We stopped and looked into each other's eyes. Then, there was another hug that lasted longer, followed by sighs, and we awkwardly broke apart. Innocence tied to titillation. I think if it had never become more, I would have been satisfied. I didn't think about the difference in our ages, and I wanted to spend time with Margery more than I wanted to do anything else. She acted as if she felt the same.

One day my father was in town getting a haircut and going over some musical scores with a business partner. I was sitting on my bed practicing my daily transcendental meditation. At that time, I was a stoner and getting high on pot and psychedelics. Some of my friends had started transcendental meditation and Kundalini yoga, so I went along with the trend. The more I practiced, the more I became pleased with the overall results in my character. Everyone was heading towards spiritual enlightenment—looking for that universal ocean of love. I needed this balance in my life, to offset the drugs. This pursuit complemented my lighter side, the part of me that wanted to be a good person, the part that wanted to be more like my brother.

I sat on my bed, cross-legged in a darkened room with my eyes closed. I focused all my attention on the third eye center of my inner mind. This daily ritual brought me peace and tranquility. The door opened, and some light entered the room. A few moments later, the door closed. It was the maid's day off and Dad wasn't home, so it had to be Margery. I thought she had come into my room looking for dishes or clothes to wash. After a few moments, the door opened again, and then closed. I didn't think anything of it and continued to meditate. A few seconds later, someone sat on the bed right next to me. Margery smelled like exotic flowers, jasmine and frangipani. Her nearness was making it difficult for me to concentrate. After a minute, something touched my hands. Fingers. Swirling. Soft, like raindrops. She slid her fingers up my arm, to my shoulder, and then to my face. I was fixed in place, nervous and afraid to open my eyes. I figured if I continued to try to meditate—I was in my safe zone.

"I am happy whenever you are near," Margery said in a soft voice.

I reached up and touched her hand, holding it gently. I brought her palm to my lips. I opened my eyes and looked into hers, glimmering green in the dim light of the room. We put our arms around each other, and it felt as though she was the first woman I had ever truly held. This hug was free of innocence and with one glance of her looking at my lips, I complemented her advance and our first kiss lasted for nearly two hours. I didn't think once about my father. I never did when I was with Margery. It was always just the two of us.

And then she was crying.

"What's wrong," I asked.

"I am happy, that's all," she said.

"And so am I," I replied. I was happy, but confused at the same time. We'd taken a step away from everything that was safe and normal. How would we ever get back? I didn't speak. I was reluctant to clutter the moment with words, but I knew that her tears, happy or not, undeniably held the future.

***

The next day, I was at a friend's house, and called home to say I wouldn't be back for dinner.

"I want to see you," Margery said.

"I'm down at Peter's."

"I want to see you in private."

"That could be arranged. The Inn is vacant."

There was a pause on the line.

"I want to hold you."

"I'm here. Peter's parents are out of town and no one else is around."

***

Two years ago, when I was thirteen, Dad had given me the sex talk. It went like this: he called me into his office and sat me down on the couch.

"You know everything there is to know about women and sex and stuff, don't you?"

"Yeah, Dad. I know everything about it."

"Okay, now you can tell your mother we had this talk."

And I was dismissed.

***

Lee thought I was worldly for my age, and I was the last person who was going to disabuse him of the notion. He saw me as a pot smoking wild child and assumed I knew everything I needed to know about women. But though I knew next to nothing about women and sex, I wasn't about to tell him that. I knew so little, that when Margery started to orgasm the first time we made love, I thought I was hurting her. I didn't even know women had orgasms.

Fortunately, I was a quick study, and learned far more than what I ever dreamed possible. That afternoon left no mysteries to elude me. Even God would have been too embarrassed to tell me what she willingly taught me. And when our encounter concluded, it would last forever in my memory as the perfect first time.

***

We came home that night, her in the jeep, and then I arrived on foot a half hour later. My father was drinking a martini beside the fireplace. Margery was perched on the edge of his sofa, ruffling his hair and kissing him. Lee cocked his head and smiled at me. I wondered if he noticed any change in her. She was warmer with him than usual, but it didn't make me jealous. Everything seemed just as it should be. My father was happy, and I was happy when my dad was happy. After showering I sat down across from Lee and read while Margery made supper.

I was too excited to feel guilty. I was on a cloud, and nothing could get to me up there. At dinner that night, Margery held Dad's hand while she played footsie with me under the table.

***

After that, she often defended herself against my father's rough, sometimes demanding nature, by taking him in her arms. I taught her that it worked better with him than confrontation. I made myself believe that it didn't matter to my father that Margery and I spent so much time together and showed open signs of affection.

***

On a typical morning, Lee read the paper and opened his mail. He'd read aloud some of the funnier stories or profound comments. Me, I'd be rolling joints. I took a few hits. He sipped from a bloody Mary. Margery was a good cook, and it didn't seem out of the ordinary that she typically created one of her epicurean wonders while wearing a short silk robe and high heels. She would tell us to close our eyes and then she'd hand-feed us syrupy pancakes. We'd all laugh like actors in a play we'd just written ourselves. Dad and I licked syrup and crumbs from Margery's fingers as she smiled and giggled.

We were constantly laughing and having fun, but, to be honest, some of those times we were all high. Nevertheless, even while sober we maintained an air of harmony about us, one that was contagious for anyone who entered our carefree sphere.

I had never wanted my parents to split—what kid does—and now I was determined to do anything to maintain family harmony between Lee and Margery. I was fifteen and wildly uninhibited. I loved Margery, and Margery loved Lee and Dad loved me and Lee loved Margery. It wasn't that I didn't know there was something strange about the setup—I just didn't care. As bizarre as that family life was, it was a happy one and I was always seeking that, the happy family life—that moment when my siblings and I waited outside my parents' bedroom on Sunday mornings for them to open the door so we could rush in and jump onto their bed. The tickling, the laughter, the love. It's what I wanted; it's what I always wanted. It was when I didn't get it that things turned upside down. Here I was, loved and happy. All I had to do was make it last.

***

Margery and I didn't have to hide our affection for each other as long as we kept it tame when Dad was around. I convinced myself that Dad was the one benefiting the most from my bond with Margery. He finally had the wife he always wanted, and he seemed to appreciate the part I was playing in that, even though he hadn't yet conceived of what it actually was. Although we all had our bearings in sight, our triangle set sail into uncharted waters; not knowing at the time there could be no return.

I felt that the more Margery and I strayed, the more love there was to go around. We compartmentalized and kept concepts of loyalty and betrayal far away. What Margery and I shared was just between the two of us, separate from anything else. For a time, Lee, Margery, and I were the three amigos. There was a balance that worked. We swam naked in the pool and spent time in the sauna. We played tricks on every other person who came into our lives.

It was 1968, a wild time, and we were wild in it. Dad played games in restaurants. He could be boisterous, pretending to lift a waitress's skirt only to get his hand slapped. Even though I was only fifteen, he bought me drinks. We were invincible. We tried to drag race with police cars, planned capers and played elaborate practical jokes on unsuspecting friends. Some of our more complex real life theatrics required the hiring of fake cops from central casting or hookers and thugs from the mean streets. As our imaginations soared to new heights, the real world became a mere playground of our own design.

Lee loved to cause a commotion. In a drunken spree, we drove downtown and Dad hung his head out of the passenger window and shouted, "Follow me. Follow me, my people." A drunk or two might look up as if the Messiah was driving down Hollywood Boulevard in a Mustang convertible and then we would speed away to the next block and do it all over again.

After dinner at Monty's Steakhouse, Dad once turned to a grim guy at the table beside us who hadn't laughed once the entire hour we'd been there.

"Want to trade wives?" Dad asked.

The stuffy diner stood up, grabbed the hand of his prudish wife, left money on the table and stomped away. Lee didn't mean to offend them, and out of respect for his fellow man, he chased them down and sincerely apologized.

The more shocking we were, the more hilarious and absurd the world became. As soon as Dad hit the fun button, we were off and running. There was no off button. The only thing that stopped us was passing out. These things happened only when no one recognized Dad. If someone did, he became the big man, the famous humanitarian, and paid for rounds of drinks for his adoring public until the wee hours of the morning.

***

I did have girlfriends my age, but they didn't interest me much. Nevertheless, I became a glutton for sex and affection from every direction. There was a blonde seventeen-year old nudist in the mountains of Aspen, who had once been my climbing partner. We now took turns climbing all over one another. On the West Coast there was the heroin addict in Brentwood. She was stoned and passed out most of the time, but her sensual divorced mother filled in downstairs while her daughter was asleep upstairs. Neither one of them minded the arrangement and gladly introduced me to the tagteam experience. It was the late sixties and love was contagious.

Margery knew about the others, and she insisted I keep up with the pretense of normalcy, whatever that may have been at the time. We knew our sexual relationship could never be exposed to the outside world, we never planned on running away, nor was it necessary. So long as our love remained our secret we were safe.

***

Lee knew that things were far better between him and Margery when I was present. He eventually asked my mother if I could come and live with them in Aspen for the second semester of my sophomore year in high school. Any time my father wanted me around I was flattered. After all, I spent half my life figuratively sitting outside his office door waiting for the moment when I could get some of his attention. Margery in the mix was an added bonus, although our times together were never planned, they just happened. We did not scheme or sneak around in silence or shame. For all of us, our unusual lifestyle was unencumbered by the technicalities of closed minds.

***

I still have the two silver chalices from the wedding with Margery's name written on one and Leon's name on the other. My reaction to their wedding wasn't what might be expected. I was having sex with my father's wife, and I didn't necessarily see this as a negative thing. I was all suited up for the happy day, and Dad was exultant. Marge was glowing, and I couldn't have been happier, because I knew that this ceremony cemented her into my life as much as into Lee's. I didn't feel rejected in the least. The marriage only made it easier for Margery and me to be together. I didn't want Margery to be in the family just so she would not run away. Although I knew if that ever happened, I might never see her again. We couldn't be together on our own as a normal adult couple. The only way I could have her was this way. Sometimes the inevitable is better, and how could I possibly complain when the world was delivered to my doorstep.

Lee insisted that Margery convert to Judaism so they could be married in a synagogue. By then, he was the poster boy for Zionism, and he may have been pandering to his public when he asked Margery to convert. As a middle name, Margery took the Hebrew name "Ariel," which means lion of God. I thought of her more as Shakespeare's Ariel, a sprite or spirit, summoned to serve Prospero, the magician. The name had a special meaning for me, and that's often how I thought of her. She was Dad's Margery, but she was my Ariel.

It wasn't a big wedding. I don't remember my brother being there, but by then, my obsession with Margery overshadowed all standard observations. Though I had so much rationalization on my side, as I watched Dad and Margery say their vows, a part of me was ashamed.

Dad stomped on the glass, and they were wed.

***

It was a new dynamic. Part of me knew what Margery and I were doing was wrong. I just didn't know which part, the good or the bad. Was I the worst son? I had dishonored my father beyond redemption, and there was no turning back. I had become the illusionist. Now I was truly like my father. I was the one writing the story now, but Lee was still the hero. The devil on one of my well-dressed shoulders and the angel on the other were both celebrating that day.

***

While Lee was deeply involved in conversation with Herb Schlosberg, his lawyer, life-long confidante and friend, Margery and I were off in the corner, sitting on a bench, concealed just enough to secretly hold hands. We watched the crowd, not each other. She squeezed my hand so tightly that I turned to look at her. She was smiling. She had what she wanted. I smiled back and then both of us stared straight ahead. It was like the last scene in *The Graduate*, which had come out the year before. When the romantic gesture is over, the couple sitting in the back of the bus suddenly realizes what they've done and the laughing stops.

4

Without Shame

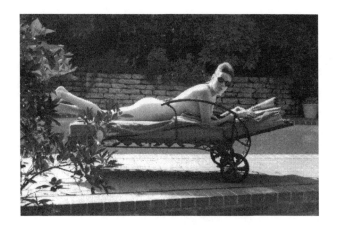

Lee was renting a house in Benedict Canyon while he worked on *Ari*, a musical based on his book *Exodus*. While Dad wrote, Margery and I shopped for this and that and went to movies and even for walks on the beach. The best times were the ones we spent with each other. It didn't matter what we were doing. Making love was only part of our mutual attraction. We took every opportunity to be together, as we considered every second a gift and the finest entertainment.

In the fall of 1968, Dad and Margery were in London to research his novel *QB VII*, based on a libel suit against him. In *Exodus*, my father had written about a Dr. Dering, a Polish war criminal who performed sterilization without anesthesia on Jews in Auschwitz. In real life, after the war, Dering went to Africa to do humanitarian work. He was eventually knighted by the Queen, and returned to England. His daughter, when she read the single sentence about her father in *Exodus*, insisted that the doctor sue my father for libel. In the end, Dering won the case but was disgraced when the British Court awarded him only a hay penny, the lowest form of currency in the realm. It was, at the time, the longest libel trial in British history. My father voluntarily paid the Derings' legal fees. Dad wanted to show his compassion for the terminally ill Dering. *QB VII* became a bestseller and the first mini-series on US television, starring Ben Gazzara as Abraham Cady (Leon Uris) and Anthony Hopkins as Dr. Adam Kelno (Doctor Dering).

***

I spent the fall semester in Los Angeles, missing Margery, but I made the best of it with my heroin addicted girlfriend and her mother. I suspected that their time alone would wear on Dad and Margery's relationship, and sure enough Betty got a letter asking me to come to London earlier than I was expected:

Dear Betty,

We heard from my secretary that Mike was booked to London on December 19th. This is very disappointing to me because I had expected him quite a bit earlier.

Margery and I planned to take him to Oxford, for example, and to the Courts and would like to do so before they go on recess and holiday. I have also booked theatre that he would miss by arriving so late.

Do you suppose you could allow him to come over earlier? I suggest that he fly out of Los Angeles on the 4th of December.

I think Mike is taking a very sensible attitude to finish his semester in Los Angeles. It will make his transfer to Aspen in February much easier for him.

I hope Karen and Mark understand that there was no favoritism involved. This is purely a case of how our relationships stand at the moment and also, quite frankly, a matter of the financial situation.

Love to the children and my deepest wishes for a happy holiday for yourself and fulfillment in the coming year.

Best, Lee

My father had made extensive travel plans for me. He wanted to show me the London courts, Oxford, and introduce me to the theater in the West End. I couldn't wait to go to England, and was excited to spend the second semester of my sophomore year in Aspen. Though my mother tried the best she could to raise me, while in Santa Monica I was unruly and stoned all the time, more than any mother could handle. So, when my father offered to mentor and take care of me, she gladly accepted.

In London, we went to see the rock-musical *Hair* that had just come out. One night I went out with Dad's London secretary's younger brother on a double date and we saw an up-and-coming group called Led Zeppelin at the Whisky A-Go-Go. Dad was always hooking me up. He wanted me to have a social life and friends my own age. We spent Christmas with Dad's Dutch publisher outside of Amsterdam. That's where I heard the Beatle's *White Album* for the first time.

Dad spent hours behind closed doors with the publisher who had been very supportive during the libel trial. This was, without a doubt, a working vacation and Dad was on a fact finding mission—doing research and preparing for his upcoming novel.

In Amsterdam, Dad, Margery and I walked through the red light district. We passed rows of women in lingerie displaying themselves in windows like dolls in boxes. Even if I had the money, I wouldn't have gone near those women, and I think Margery and Lee knew it. The women, smiling though they were, seemed lacking in the affectionate type of love I required.

Back in London, we stayed at the flat Lee had rented. We were on the first floor of a three-story townhouse in Central London. When Dad was out working, Margery and I ambled around London together. When Dad was free, we all went into the countryside looking for antiques. Margery fit right into rural England, and people fell all over themselves to please her, they knew a rare treasure when they found one. We had a grand old time, drinking, eating, laughing, and sleeping in until eleven every other day, but nothing stopped my father from continuing his busy schedule.

This was one of the most passionate times of my life. Margery and I somehow knew what to do to make each other happy and I was grateful for every moment that we had together. As usual we never snuck around, and my father gave us those times together, and that fact alone made our triangle most unusual. My sense of romance was so acute, I believed the feeling I had for Margery would never end and, at the same time, I knew that inevitably, it had to. As for her feelings and my father's, I will never know the entire truth.

On New Year's Eve, the three of us stayed in, and Dad and I had a drinking contest. We each had two bottles of champagne and the one who finished first won. I gave it my best shot, then spent the rest of the evening throwing up. It could have been a set-up. Dad knew I'd do whatever it took to win, and I'd end up incapacitated leaving him alone with Margery.

Hell, it was all in good fun.

***

At the end of January, I joined Dad and Margery in Aspen for the second semester of the tenth grade. My mother was worried because I was so out of control, but my father promised he'd keep a close eye on me. Even then, I knew that I served a function in my dad's life. His relationship with Margery was unraveling after they returned from London, and my presence would break the tension. I had only been away from them for three weeks, but even that had taken a toll on their relationship.

Lee and Margery were both there to pick me up at the airport in Aspen. We went home and had dinner. Margery had learned to make a traditional matzo ball soup. She was trying to be a good Jewish wife. She was withdrawn and quiet that evening. She waited until the two of us were washing the dishes before she told me what was bothering her.

"I think your dad is beginning to suspect something," she said, her chin lowered, her hands reaching into the sink. "He knows I'm miserable when you're not around."

"How does he know?"

"I think he knows the way I feel about you."

"Did you tell him that you're sleeping with me?"

"He knows. He just knows, because when he touches me it's just not the same."

"The same as what?"

"He tries. But we're just not happy in that way—exually. He blames me."

"Was it wrong for me to be here? Is it a mistake?" I reached for her hand in the soapy water.

"Not as far as I'm concerned, but I think your father brought you here for a reason—and it's not for the one you thought." She took her hands out of the water, wiped them on a dishtowel and let the water drain. She took the lotion she kept next to the sink and rubbed it into her hands. It made the kitchen smell like lemon.

"My relationship with Dad is great. I couldn't imagine it being better," I said.

"He does like having you around."

"Then, what's the problem?"

"You know how calculating he is. I think he wants revenge."

"Should I go back to California?" It wasn't as if I intended to turn around then and there, and fly back halfway across the country. I didn't want to leave, but I would have to take heed of her warning.

"Maybe he just needs time to readjust." She turned to me. "I could just be imagining things."

"Have you been arguing?"

"It's getting worse every day. At times, we can't even sit at the table together. You know how he is—his eyes turn red, and he looks at me in disgust. He's hanging out in town with Walt Smith."

"Doing what?"

"He says he's working on the musical, but I think he's just floating around Walt's bar. Your father is definitely avoiding me."

"You think he's seeing other women?"

"It's crossed my mind. I think when your father looks at me now, he sees you there, and he becomes enraged with jealousy. And when I look at him, I also see you, the similarities between you. I think he knows I'm in love with you."

A coffee cup fell out of my hand and hit the floor with a bump, but it didn't break. My heart was beating fast and I steadied myself against the counter. Pure panic. My perfect triangle was out of whack and I had to put it right, but I didn't see how I could. Margery was jumpy and I could tell she knew it was the beginning of the end.

5

The Vault

I was hoping that my father was just going through one of his cold phases. Meals were eaten in silence and there was no laughter, but while we maintained a semblance of normality, he was spinning a web and drawing us into it.

The day before my sixteenth birthday, Margery decided to drive up the Roaring Fork valley, claiming to my father that she needed to shop for a present. Along the way she stopped and liberated me from my science class. When we reached Glenwood Springs, we slipped into a room she had reserved in advance. She got out of the car first, registered and retrieved the key. Then, I slipped in after her. It was a tacky motel on the way out of town. There was no one else around. Drab and basic with a drab yellow bedspread. We immediately pulled the curtains. We sat on the edge of the bed and held hands. She didn't look at me at first. Eventually, we held each other, but there was desperation in it. On the way to the motel we'd talked about a possible scenario with my father. I worried about Lee's temper, what he might say to Margery. I couldn't stand it when he yelled at her and I suspected he was orchestrating some kind of psychodrama around my birthday.

"I'm almost certain your father wants to end the marriage," Margery said.

"What would you do?"

"Don't worry about me. I have friends. They'll help me. I might go back east. But I might not be able to see you, not for a long time. We need to be together. We need to be together today."

She was so passionate that afternoon, but the tears of joy that were always there when we made love had turned to tears of sorrow. She held onto me so hard, she bruised my back and arms, a death grip. A big change was coming; I just didn't know what it was. I knew this was the last time we'd be together for a long time. I felt love, but also emptiness.

At first, everything had been so bright. We were lost in

amazement and now it was as if someone had turned the lights out and we were wandering through the dark. Nothing felt good anymore. I felt desperate as I scrambled for a way to put things back to the way they were before.

We had meant only to spend the afternoon together, but when we returned to Aspen our love had changed into something too powerful to be disguised. We were exposed.

"No matter what happens, I'll always love you," Margery said as she got out of the car.

***

I did not see Margery that night at dinner, which was strange. My father told me that she felt under the weather and wanted to rest. His eyes shifted around the kitchen. He could barely look at me. Fortunately, we had a television to distract us, even though it was black and white with only one station. We finished our meal without conversation. After dinner, Dad kissed me goodnight, as he always did.

"I'll pick you up after school tomorrow and we'll go to the music store, buy you some music for your birthday."

He had never picked me up from school before and he hated my taste in music.

"Great," I said. "Thank you." Acting as though I was just a normal kid on the evening before his sixteenth birthday, how distorted could my life have been. This was the world of illusion I now resided in.

I didn't see Margery the next morning and assumed she slept in late with my father. He picked me up after school, as planned, and we went to the small record store in town. The albums were $2.99 then, and I selected ten of them.

"Get whatever you want, Son. This is your day," Dad said. He dropped me off and went to do an errand. He came back a half hour later to pay for the albums. Dad was preoccupied, but then he often was. "Want to go to the Red Onion for your birthday tonight?"

"That would be great. What time?" He didn't answer. "Seven? Eight o'clock?" I asked.

After a pause, he said, "Eight."

"How is Margery today? Is she feeling better?"

"Yes. She's fine. She's looking forward to dinner."

After finishing my homework, I began to listen to my new records. I rolled a joint and started to get stoned. At about seven, my father appeared at my bedroom door. He came in and handed me a beer.

"I just opened it. You can drink the rest," he said. This wasn't unusual. He'd often pop a beer in front of me and hand it off. What was strange was that this time the beer was already opened. "I'll collect you for dinner in about a half hour. You can turn up the music. Crank it up."

After he left, I took a sip of the beer. It was flat and barely cool. I sniffed it. It didn't smell right. I had stolen Dad's sleeping pills on a regular basis. I'd opened the capsules and snorted the drug. I recognized the smell and taste. The beer my father gave me was spiked.

This birthday dinner was never going to happen. I hadn't seen Margery for a day and a half. I loaded up the record player with a few albums, turned up the volume and then followed my father down the hallway.

Our house was halfway up Red Mountain, two miles from town on a narrow, steep, curving road. There was a breathtaking panoramic view of the town and surrounding mountain peaks from any window in the house. It was snowing and already dark so the wise residents of Red Mountain were hunkered down inside.

***

My father went directly to his office, which was in a building separate from the main house. I looked around for Margery. She was not in the kitchen, or bedroom, or living room or library. It was then that I opened the window and looked toward my father's office. Giant snowflakes were falling and blanketing the hill. The garage door opened (the garage was under the office) and one of the jeeps started. Dad came down from his office, opened the door of the jeep, grabbed Margery and pulled her out of the driver's seat. Margery was dressed for the cold and Dad was wearing a cotton undershirt, a long sleeved flannel Pendleton and après-ski boots.

"You cannot take one of my cars! If you want to leave, you'll have to walk," he yelled. Margery pulled away from him and began to walk down the driveway. He followed her, jabbing the air with his finger, and screaming profanities. Margery kept walking away from him. Once, she stopped for just a second, glanced up at the house, and, looking directly at me, she gently waved, her hand at chest height, a subtle acknowledgment that she knew I was there. Then, she turned and continued to walk with my father following behind her, kicking up snow.

I figured we'd been spotted in Glenwood Springs. That would be bad, but what would be worse was if Margery had finally had enough of my father's anger and confessed the truth.

Arriving at the main road that led to town, Lee and Margery were lit by a streetlight at the end of the driveway; two characters acting out a violent play. My father blocked the way to town, and Margery began to walk backward up the hill. This was the moment. Either I had to become a man or remain a fictionalized projection of my father's will. The decision was clear. I stopped at the entrance closet on my way to the front door, took one of the loaded handguns from the shelf, and placed it in my back pocket. This was not a cap gun like the one I carried into my father's office at age four, this was a deadly weapon, and this time logic eluded me as anger set in. I was prepared to use it on my father if he transformed into a demon.

In only shorts, a tee shirt and high-topped tennis shoes with thick knee-high wool socks, I hastened my journey through the ankle deep snow.

***

Once my father and Margery left the glow of artificial light from the house, the darkness enveloped them. On this stretch of the hillside, there were only two homes—my father's and the other one appeared to be empty. The snowflakes were as large as dimes and created their own shadowy light source. The dense snowflakes shifted, and the ghostly images continued to move away from the house. My father's yelling and Margery's crying broke the silence. I couldn't make out Lee's exact words, but even from a distance, I could feel his rage.

Margery tried to fight back, but she was no match for Leon Uris. He'd been honing his language all his life. He was relentless. Even after he'd crushed her like an eggshell, he continued to pulverize her. I wanted to grab Dad, pull him back, to stop him, even if it meant knocking him out. I pleaded with my conscience for the gun to remain in my back pocket, but it seemed as though my father had already transformed into a powerful demon. There was no wind. The snowflakes drifted. Gentle Margery faced my unyielding father and I ran toward them. I could barely see a few steps ahead of me.

"Enough. Enough already," I said.

Dad turned toward me. "So, my backstabbing piss-head of a son arrives right on schedule."

"Stop attacking Margery," I said.

"Go back to the house. Leave us alone," he said.

"Face it. You planned on me following you. You left clues."

Margery took a handkerchief out of her purse, wiped some tears away, and blew her nose. I walked up closer to the two of them. We all faced one another, creating the corners of what was once our perfect triangle.

"Clever," my father said.

I wiped the snow from my tennis shoes. "Right. I got it. The albums. Picking me up at school, the spiked beer. None of it was normal. You tricked me, leaving clues that made no sense, yet you knew I would be intrigued enough to follow. It's fucking cold and wet out here. If you wanted to ruin my birthday, you could have at least dumped your shit on me by the fireplace. I knew something was wrong. Margery was gone all day. Was there something you didn't want her to tell me? What the fuck is going on, Dad?"

Dad laughed like the phantom of the opera. "You're an idiot, Son. Keep guessing."

Margery lowered her head. I stood in the snow, helpless.

"I didn't know what you wanted at first, but now I do. You wanted to enrage me. Well, you've done it. You have your audience now and the players have all arrived. Let's begin the show," I said.

My father remained silent.

Margery looked at me, a sad expression on her face. "Lee and I, it just isn't working out. I don't know which way to turn. If I choose your father, I lose you. If I choose you, I lose your father. He knows about yesterday. Someone saw us."

Dad pointed his forefinger at Margery. "I saw the presents you bought for Mike and you had the nerve to tell me you were going to buy gifts that I knew you had already wrapped. Then you drive down valley to do what? And Susie sees you and Mike on a school day heading out of town."

Margery stared at Dad, and then turned to me.

"Lee confronted me before dinner yesterday and I didn't lie. I can't lie anymore. I'm sorry, Michael." She turned back to Dad. "Your father had no intention of going out to dinner. He's ashamed of you and of me and of himself for allowing us to carry on as long as we did."

"Would things get any better between the two of you if I walked away? You know I never meant to hurt you. For once in my life I take full responsibility. I take responsibility for ruining your marriage."

"She's the one who came on to you." Dad raised his voice. "But you're no better than her," he said pointing that crooked finger of death at me. "Your brother would never stab me in the back like this."

"My brother didn't fall in love with Margery. I did. We are way past who is to fucking blame. Falling in love just happens. Is it immoral to love someone? Is it wrong to want to be near them? When you fell in love with Margery, did you have any choice? No. And neither did I, so don't tell me I stabbed you in the back. I was right in front of you. We were face-to-face when I stabbed you in the heart."

Dad shook his head. "I'm so disgusted with you. Both of you."

Margery said, "I need both of you."

"We all need each other. Dad conveniently forgets his own anger. He thinks he is clean in all of this. If we even try to confront him, he just turns his back on us. You shouldn't have to live in fear of his shit, his red devil eyes and his anger. He thinks I should grow up. Well, I think he regressed back to some sick shit from his childhood!"

"You're certainly the family expert on shit! You're so full of it," Dad yelled.

I pointed at my father the same way he pointed at me. "Look at yourself, the grand manipulator and I am your crowning achievement." I lowered my hand. "I enjoy being Frankenstein's monster. That's the only way I could get an audience with the good doctor. All I ever wanted was to be in your good graces; whatever happened between Margery and me was not part of my plan. But your grand design collapsed. You lost control of me, your wife and of yourself. You've had your failures, Dad, accept it, I'm one of them."

Dad shook his head and glanced down as Margery looked on. "You don't know me at all."

I could tell Dad was headed into one of his orations. That's what he did—often. He didn't talk. He gave speeches. It was as if he exploded with them. And I learned from him.

I laid my cards on the table. "Look up at me, Dad. You always look down. I struggle to be like you. I idealize you. I follow you through every stinking passageway. I know where you go. Could anyone know you better than me? I'm your fucking son. With one hand you raise something up, but to do that, you always have to condemn the other side. You secretly praise your adversary, because without them, you would be an ordinary man and nothing scares you more than that. I know how badly your parents crippled you and you've been running away from who you really are ever since. You joined the Marines during WWII just to get away from your own father. You chanced dying in combat to keep from having to sit down with your father at the dinner table. Would you even recognize the real Leon Uris if you ran into him on the street? You created me in your own image. I know what's in your heart. I only have to go as far as the nearest mirror to find you."

"Your son loves you." Margery sat down in the snow with her arms hugging her knees.

Dad looked into my eyes. "Maybe you do know me."

"And I care about you, but I have to start every day by breaking the mold, by assuring myself that I'm my own person, not just an extension of you."

"Nicely played, Son. Maybe I taught you too well. No matter how much you fight it, you'll never be a model citizen—you'll never be like your brother. You are my black rose."

Even under such stress, in the snow, in the dark, my father could write his dialogue and hurl the crippling words like weapons.

Margery stayed seated there in the cold, hugging her knees and rocking back and forth.

"Nice back hand, Dad. You can piss me off if you want, but you can insult me from now until the day I die and I'll never love you less.

I'm no fucking angel and I fucked up and I screwed my father and I screwed the woman he loves. But the truth is, Margery is much more than either of us deserve."

Now we were both looking at Margery. Her pale smile glistened in the snow. Neither of us deserved to look at her then. She was so full of love and we were an angry pair, squared off against each other and I know I was ashamed for her to see me like that, and I think Dad was as well. Margery stood up, walked over to my father, and touched his arm. She smiled when he looked at her. Then, she walked over to me and touched my arm and smiled at me. Then, she took a few steps back and resumed her position in the triangle.

"I know I am the one who is out of line. The only solution is for me to walk down that road and give you and Margery a fair chance. It has to be that way," I said.

"Look, if you didn't love Margery as much as she loves you, we wouldn't be in this mess," Lee said. "Now you know what really bothers me, it is your love for her. Her love for you might fade, but I feel your love for her will never go away."

I shivered in the cold. "Why can't we go on the way it is? Why do you suddenly need to be conventional? You always taught me to be the opposite. Who cares whose name is on a piece of paper if we all love each other? It's been working. It works. I think deep down you understood what was going on all along. You gave us the time together. Why can't we both love her?"

He turned away and shook his head. He stomped his feet, either from cold or frustration. "What a mess," he said.

I was out there without gloves and I banged my hands together to warm them up. "This is the higher ideal. Don't you see it? You're the one who taught it to me."

"I can never be that understanding."

"Dad, you can't see past your anger and you'll let it destroy all of us. At least I know where to draw the line. At least I know when to stop."

"You think so, do you?"

"I only allow my anger to destroy my own castle made of sand. I don't telegraph anger into the hearts of others. I'm not like you."

Dad brushed snow from his hair. "You put your faith in a role model who simply doesn't exist. That image was misplaced long ago." Dad knew he wasn't getting anywhere with me. Whereas someone else might have chosen that moment to walk away, Dad readied his heavy verbal artillery. This combat veteran wasn't about to back down.

"We can build our castle on higher ground," I said. I could see the future and I didn't like it, Margery going away, me going back to Los Angeles in disgrace.

"I only wish that were possible." Dad looked down at Margery. "She sacrificed more than you know, for you, Son. To be with me, and with you, she gave up her chance to have children."

I knew that she'd had a tubal operation. I thought to myself, what did that have to do with me?

"Michael, you didn't know I was pregnant." Margery dropped to her knees and started to cry. "I'm not certain it was your father's child."

At first I didn't know what she meant, but then it hit me. Margery had had an abortion and that child, the one my father made sure was destroyed, was possibly not his. I walked up to my father and shoved him off balance.

I asked, "So, you knew about this? You allowed me to be with her all these months. Why, out of guilt from the blood on your hands? You're a fucking asshole!"

"Look at you? Who has lost control now?" Dad stared at me with purple eyes.

I reached back as far as I could, swung my hand around and slapped my father across the face. Dad's head snapped to the side.

"I deserved that," Lee said. "And you deserve better." He hurled his fist forward and hit me squarely on the jaw. The force thrust me backwards onto the snow. Marge yelled for us to stop. It took me a minute to get to my feet and brush off the snow. I must have looked like I'd been rolled in flour and the snow kept coming. I rubbed my jaw. Lee really knew how to cold-cock a guy. He really put his weight into it.

I faced her. "Whatever happened with the operation, it could never change the way I feel about you."

"I can't keep secrets anymore," she said. "What we had, you and I, was always our own," she said. "What Lee and I had was something different." Margery was telling me she loved me, and doing it in front of my father. It was bold, bold for all of us, but to me, it justified everything I had done.

"Happy birthday, Son. You fucked up her life, my life, and your own and you accomplished it all before you turned sixteen."

"It's too late to change what has already happened," Margery said.

Dad pointed at me again with his hooked finger. "Understand this. There are limits to everyone's tolerance. Raising someone else's child was mine."

Margery's expression broke my heart.

I turned to my father. "You can do whatever you want to me," I said, my voice cracking, "But when you destroy her—I just can't stand it!" I turned my back on him. "I have no father!"

"Good! I don't recognize you as my son!" He came around me, got right up into my face and pointed at his chin. He might as well have said, 'Hit me.'

I caught him on the jaw. It wasn't a hard blow. He didn't even sway. Then I rushed him, hitting him low and lifting him up with my shoulder. We were football players, and he was the one who taught me how to take someone down. We wrestled violently in the snow, throwing wild punches, swearing. Headlocks and twisting arms and legs. He rubbed my face in the snow and I spit it out in his face. Something was keeping me from hitting his face, deep inside I knew this fight was wrong, and it only made sense to lessen the blows.

My father felt no such compunction. He continued to try to beat me senseless. Throwing all his body weight behind his punches, he pounded on my chest until I heard my ribs crack, and I felt such pain I had never known before. But it was pain from a broken heart that really hurt, from the loss of my father; both of us had crossed the line to which there was no return. Lee was so out of control, I almost felt ashamed for him, for his inability to harness his anger. There was no restraining his aggression. This was his way of venting months of frustration. I counter-attacked insult for insult, taking the obscenities he yelled at me and turning them right back at him. That only made him more furious and he stepped up his physical assault. I finally realized there was no chance to stop him, so I resorted to the next level of violence, pulling the gun out of my pocket and pointing it at his chest. I wasn't about to cry uncle; I was my father's son, and to stop short of winning was never an option.

When my father saw the gun, he put both his hands on it and drew it closer to his chest. I released the gun and Dad tossed it into the snow.

"Now Margery knows what a lunatic you can be."

"I never pulled the trigger," I said.

"You're no different from me. I might have had to drag that level of anger out of you, but I always knew it was there behind the facade. And now Margery knows, too."

I was lying in the snow and started to clap. "Great performance, Dad. Now, I understand what this is all about. You wanted to show her that I was as out of control as you. Good show." I stumbled up.

We were back in our corners.

Lee said, "There is no way out for any of us. We are all broken. My own son broke me. You think I was controlling you, but that's just an illusion. Each of us controlled our own lives."

Margery looked up at us. "We were real. What we had was real. This isn't real, this is nothing more than a beautiful dream gone bad."

Dad hugged himself for warmth as he continued his assault. "I want both of you to suffer right along with me. Do you feel the intensity of my pain—do you even care? No matter where you go in this world may what little guilt you have drive you insane! No one's innocent here. I can't hide from my own conscience for forcing you together. That's the worst part."

"You could have stopped us, at any point along the way, but you were afraid we'd both leave you if you did," I said.

"In the beginning, I never wanted to hurt you, Mike. I never wanted to hurt you, Margery. I never wanted either of you to be unhappy, but I didn't want you to be so happy that you wouldn't need me anymore. Over the last year I put up with a lot. I don't think there was any evil intent, not for either of you. Tonight, I need you to understand that I'm totally disgusted with you and you probably feel the same way about me. You are right about one thing: I do manipulate people, but I did not spend the last few months trying to ruin your lives. I wanted to fix it. I wanted to fix it all. I tried, but I just couldn't do it." He kneeled down across from Margery and put his hands on her shoulders. "From the first time I saw you, I knew it was impossible for you to actually cherish me. I could fool you with my celebrity and charm only long enough to get you to fall in love with me. Even my son knew that my anger and impatience would eventually overshadow all the decency in me. It took less time than I thought for me to break down—only a few months and I was sniping at you—shooting down your self-confidence. I had no more chance of keeping you happy than I had of controlling you." He reached out and touched Margery's face. "You never did get rid of that mole."

My father had made several inquiries about Margery's beauty mark to a plastic surgeon in Beverly Hills. As beautiful as she was, he wanted to change her.

"I wanted to keep it. It's part of me," Margery said.

"You were stronger than I imagined you'd be, but the first time you looked away from me in disgust, I should have taken that message to heart," Dad stood and faced me. "And Mike, I actually enjoyed beating you." He looked down. "And I'm not ashamed of it. We should end this before anyone else gets hurt."

"Why don't you let Margery decide what she wants to do?" I said.

"She had her chance," Dad replied.

"Why not take some of that tolerance and compassion that you put into your books and public image, and give it to those who are closest to you? You are pushing her out the door. You're the one who is abandoning her, not the other way around. Just know that."

"This isn't about abandonment, it's about betrayal."

"You're acting like a coward," Margery said without looking up.

My father leaned down, reached into the snow, and retrieved the handgun he had tossed away, and gave it to Margery.

"You want to make a choice? Then make one, but I will not change. You can stay, but you can't have my son as your consolation prize. Do me a big favor and shoot me, or get out of my life."

Margery pointed the gun at Lee. She was shaking and so was the gun.

"Don't think I don't love you, Lee. I love you both. Don't use the love Michael and I have as an excuse to ruin his life. He still looks up to you." Still shaking, she lowered the gun.

"Jealousy is a beast and it tracked me down. I can't get rid of it without getting rid of the love that goes with it." My father shook his head. "I'm helpless to control this rage. My father molded my image as a child. And when I turned to my father for answers, of why my mother made me wait outside the door as she entertained the strangers, my father became enraged with jealousy. Me being only a child, the image of my father crying imprinted upon my mind. What you see, and all that stands before you, is not the fictional image I created out of necessity. I live in constant fear of becoming an emotional cripple like my father."

I looked at my father. "I look up to you, but don't repeat the mistakes of your father and expect me to follow."

I knelt, reached out and touched Margery's cheek, wet with tears. "There was no happy ending to this and everyone always knew it. It wasn't like you and I could ever make it on our own. We were three. We could never survive, just the two of us."

Margery continued to weep.

I stood up and faced my father. "I was selfish. You are bitter. Tonight, both of us lost more than we thought possible. And Margery is trapped in the middle. You're right all along; we were only pretending to exist in a perfect world. But isn't that what we do best? Why does continuing to live in an imaginary world have to end in ruin?"

Dad reached out and held my shoulder. "I'm sorry."

"It doesn't have to be this way," I said.

Lee faced his wife and shook his head. "We're done." He added, "Forgive me."

"No," she whispered. With the gun in her hand, Margery stood up. She started to walk away. Then, she began to run.

My father stood where he was, but I ran after her up the hill. I could only see a vague shadow of her in the dark. When I got closer, I pleaded with her to come back. I made a few positive statements, refusing to let her believe the contrary, saying that things might be better in the morning, after everyone has had time to let things settle. She was sobbing and still holding the gun in one hand, her purse with the other.

I reached for the gun, but my hand slipped off her clothing and the gun discharged. I wondered what the hell was going on. Why was she still holding the gun? Terrified, I reached out again into the darkness. The gun discharged a second time—so loud on the quiet mountain. I could see her through the dim light. She raised the gun to her mouth. I took hold of her arm and tried to pull the gun away, but she held firm. Her hand was locked in place. I was afraid resisting her might force her to make the wrong decision, so I loosened my grip. There was no right decision. It was her choice. I knew what was coming next. She stopped crying and looked into my eyes. That was the last time I saw her alive. All the love was there—the sweetness, the passion, and even the remorse that I alone would have to bare.

All I could hear was the two of us breathing.

And then the sound of a shot echoed throughout the night.

On the hillside by the side of the road, sitting on a blanket of snow, I held her motionless body. Wailing, tears streamed from my eyes.

6

What Remained

My wailing ceased and I went into shock. I heard my father's voice screaming in the distance, but I did not answer. A few minutes later he was standing by my side. We were all covered in falling snow and resembled ghosts in the darkness. Lee looked at me holding Margery. My father touched my shoulder to comfort me. He did not pay me the courtesy of being relieved that I was still alive. Some things were better left unsaid.

"I heard three shots," he whispered.

I looked up to him. Tears streamed from his eyes. He lowered his head and cried. A couple of minutes later, Dad found her purse and opened it. There was another handgun inside. She had taken one with her when she left the house. He said, "A second gun. She never intended on going into town. Son, I never..."

"Neither did I," I interrupted. "Leave me with her. You owe me that much."

I continued to hold her, not wanting to let her go. I should have been shivering from the cold, but I wasn't because of the shock. My face was caked with snow and tears. If it were up to me I would have stayed there until I froze.

My father took off his outer shirt and slipped it over my shoulders. I desperately tried to throw the blame upon him, but my conscience would not allow it. Even though neither one of us pulled the trigger, in our own ways, we were equally to blame.

Dad pried my fingers and then my arms away from her. It seemed as though I had held her for an eternity. I was in shock and numb from the cold, and even if I wanted to, I could barely move. Dad dragged me up the embankment to the road. He left me there and went back to Margery where he made a few adjustments to the scene. He wanted to hide the fact that I'd ever been there. The falling snow would cover any remaining evidence of my involvement, as if it really mattered to me at all. My father understood the complexity of being involved with a violent death, apparent suicide or not. Returning, he lifted me over his shoulder and carried me down the roadway, one methodic step after another. He slipped a couple of times and we both tumbled into snowdrifts, but my father was determined to bring his son home and he carried me every inch of the way.

Dad put me in a cold bath and slowly raised the temperature. After thawing out, he helped me into warm clothes and fed me a few tranquilizers and muscle relaxers. Then, he left the room to make a phone call. He came back a few minutes later. He and his lawyer had decided that the best move was to do whatever was necessary to make sure neither of us was implicated in the tragedy. This was a private family matter. My father would stand between public ridicule and my future—our futures. I don't know if he did this for my benefit or to salvage his reputation, yet after the suicide of a wife how could the sharks not thrive on a merciless feeding frenzy.

All I had to say was that I'd been listening to records while I waited to go out to dinner. Dad's story was that he got into an argument with Margery and refused to let her take the car. She walked away and later he heard three shots. He thought Margery might be shooting at the house. He looked out the window to see if he could find her and then he went to check on me in my room. After that, he became concerned about Margery and called the sheriff.

***

A few minutes later, the sheriff arrived at the house and my father and I both got in the backseat of his station wagon. We drove around with him for a while pretending to look for Margery, but the heavy snow had covered our tracks. We only looked down the hill. The sheriff figured she was headed toward town. He never thought to look above the house. I'm not sure what he thought of me in my near catatonic state. He knew it was my birthday. Maybe he thought I was just disappointed that our planned celebration had gone awry. The sheriff couldn't have possibly imagined what had actually happened.

I wore a turtleneck and hat to cover the bruises on my neck, chin, and head, souvenirs of the fight with my father. Before the sheriff came, my dad wrapped my ribs with ace bandages, but it still hurt to breathe. The tranquilizers and muscle relaxers helped ease my nerves and breathing.

***

Two days later this article appeared in a Colorado newspaper:

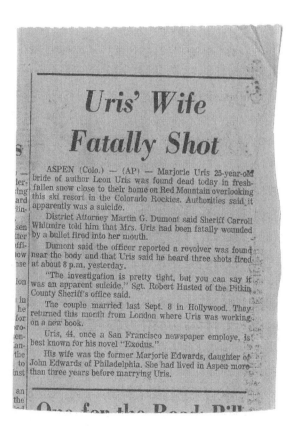

Uris' Wife Fatally Shot

ASPEN (Colo.) — (AP) — Marjorie Uris 25-year-old bride of author Leon Uris was found dead today in fresh-fallen snow close to their home on Red Mountain overlooking this ski resort in the Colorado Rockies. Authorities said it apparently was a suicide.

District Attorney Martin G. Dumont said Sheriff Carroll Whitmire told him that Mrs. Uris had been fatally wounded by a bullet fired into her mouth.

Dumont said the officer reported a revolver was found near the body and that Uris said he heard three shots fired at about 8 p.m. yesterday.

"The investigation is pretty tight, but you can say it was an apparent suicide," Sgt. Robert Husted of the Pitkin County Sheriff's office said.

The couple married last Sept. 8 in Hollywood. They returned this month from London where Uris was working on a new book.

Uris, 44, once a San Francisco newspaper employe, is best known for his novel "Exodus."

His wife was the former Marjorie Edwards, daughter of John Edwards of Philadelphia. She had lived in Aspen more than three years before marrying Uris.

ASSOCIATED PRESS HEADLINES: "Uris' Wife Fatally Shot
ASPEN (Colorado)—(AP)—Marjorie Uris 25-year-old bride of
author Leon Uris was found dead today in fresh fallen snow close to their
home on Red Mountain overlooking this ski resort in the Colorado Rockies.
Authorities said it apparently was a suicide.

> *District Attorney Martin G. Dumont said Sheriff Carroll Whitmire*
told him that Mrs. Uris had been fatally wounded by a bullet fired into her
mouth.

> *Dumont said the officer reported a revolver was found near the body*
and that Uris said he heard three shots fired at about 8 p.m. yesterday.

> *"The investigation is pretty tight, but you can say it was an apparent*
suicide," Sgt. Robert Husted of the Pitkin County Sheriff's office said.

> *The couple married last September 8th in Hollywood. They returned*
this month from London where Uris was working on a new book.

> *Uris, 44, once a San Francisco newspaper employee, is best known for*
his novel EXODUS.

> *His wife was the former Margery Edwards, daughter of John*
Edwards of Philadelphia. She had lived in Aspen more than three years
before marrying Uris."

***

I didn't sleep that night, and to maintain normalcy Dad insisted
I attend school the next morning. At school I ditched my classes
and hid behind the bleachers in the gym. Shortly before 11:00
a deputy arrived at the school to fetch me home. I remember
hearing my name broadcast on the school PA system, "Will Michael
Uris please come to the principal's office." I knew Margery's body
had been found. Welcome to my typical day. My existence absurd,
my father disgusted with me, and my lover dead. Even though I
ruled in my world of imagination, I would have to accept my destiny
like an immovable object.

***

During the inquest, my father's lawyers said that any information I could offer was insignificant. I was traumatized by the event, even more so because it happened on my sixteenth birthday, and was under heavy sedation. The family doctor backed that up with his report.

Lee's version of events prevailed. The only thing Dad left out was our confrontation on the hillside, and the yearlong affair, and the fact he tried to destroy my life and hers on my birthday. But other than that, his story was as close to the truth as a fictional author could possibly be. I didn't care what he told the world. It wouldn't change what happened on that mountain. I only had Lee to turn to for support. And I only had him to turn to for some form of vengeance. It was my father who stood between me, and the edge of existence, even though he was the one who had driven me to it. Some things never change around the Uris household.

***

During her funeral service at the house, I was heavily sedated. Weakened, I had not eaten any solid food since the incident and feared sleep. Even so, it was only a few seconds after I was seated, before I completely lost it, broke down and cried. Those who filled the living room of our Aspen house, my father's Jewish lawyer who performed the service, and everyone in attendance, realized at the same moment the intensity of my grief. For the first time since her death, the outside world got a glimpse at some of the real harm that was done. If one picture is worth a thousand words, in those few moments an epic tragedy was written. I remember their tears and sighs as I was respectfully escorted up the stairs to my father's room. There, I slept on a portable bed, where my father kept a close eye on me since the night of her death. I never denied that Dad cared more about me than I was capable of understanding.

Lee came to me sometime after the service. He sat on the edge of the bed and he hugged me and told me that Margery loved me and that was all I ever had to remember. With the utmost sincerity in his voice he clarified that her death was mainly his fault since he had given her nowhere to turn. He had realized months before that the marriage was doomed. He actually tried to make it work—his desperation kept me in her life—the only buffer between them that ever worked—the only chance for their marriage to survive, but in the end, consumed by his own frustration and rage, he could no longer deal with the jealousy and betrayal that he himself created. Poetic irony made this tragedy the most profound experience of our life together, and neither one of us would ever be the same.

This night, my father held me for the longest time. He broke down and cried, and begged for my forgiveness. I firmly rejected his plea in honor of the woman that I loved. In remorse for causing her death tears flowed from my eyes. I begged for my father's forgiveness and in memory of his wife, he rejected my plea. What he did say was, someone we both loved died by our own hands and for that there could never be absolution. The best we can do is go on with our lives.

Then, my father sealed the entrance to the vault and he stated, that if our relationship had any chance of surviving, we could never say her name. No one understood his words better than I did. His intent was clear, but it was not mine. I needed to recognize her as the angel who touched our lives, an inspiration that filled our days with perfection.

Some tears are destined to last forever. Although my father's heart was broken, his insensitivity and anger were largely responsible for her death, and this evening, as with the night of her suicide, the words he felt necessary and justified should have never been spoken.

***

An exquisite oil painting of Margery, previously commissioned by Lee, hung in the library of my father's home in Aspen. After Margery's passing, I was drawn to the portrait, sometimes spending hours in front of it. What I wanted from the masterfully portrayed likeness was to be in the company of my friend, and to remember her.

***

My father passed on over a decade ago. I cried crocodile tears at his funeral, mainly to keep up appearances. To this day, I still anticipate the time when I will finally break down and cry, as surely as I love my father, this experience will come. Someone who is that much a part of you never fades. In my world of imagination he never died, and his spirit remains right by my side. He is here with me as I type these words. In the real world he is gone. For far too long, only I knew what transpired that tragic night. Over the years I told family and friends a hundred different fabrications of what really happened. Now that my father is gone, there is no one left to share that experience with. That burden is the greatest I have ever carried. What she found in my father and my despicable self baffles me to this day. I am only left with the comfort of remembering the love we shared, and in my imagination that love today is the same as when we first held one another.

Throughout the years, Margery has remained an undeniable light in my life. Her splendor, grace and unsurpassed beauty, the sweetness of her wit and charm, her passion, the kindness of her soul, a serenity that encompassed her being, and the perfection of her every expression shall always be locked away safely in my heart. It has not been easy facing the world knowing I can never look in her eyes and feel the warmth of her love.

On a cold winter afternoon my father and I, along with family and friends, skied down the face of Aspen Mountain. Each one of us carried a plastic bag containing Margery's cremated remains. It was a sad day and few words were spoken. My father never once looked at me and smiled. Instead, we both lowered our heads in shame. From being closer together than ever before, as father and son, we were now farther apart than if we'd lived on opposite ends of the universe.

7

Out of Control

During the few months that followed Margery's death, I continued to sleep on the cot in my father's room. Lee, who was dealing with remorse and depression, frequently slipped out of Aspen and headed east to ostensibly do research for his novel, *QB VII*. I believe his visits to the Mayo Clinic's Psychiatry Department to do thorough research on the workings of an Auschwitz surgeon's guilty conscience, had more to do with his own guilt over the death of Margery than he led anyone to believe. Since the antagonist in all of his novels were allegorical versions of his own alter ego, it wasn't difficult to understand the real reason for his frequent trips to the Mayo Clinic. Lee identified with his characters, and this one in particular.

Though Dad and I kept a close eye on each other, it was hard for the two of us to face one another. I was better off when Lee was away. When we were together, he flat out refused to bring up Margery's name and that really tore me up. Living with a father who could not face the truth, or even his own son, was painful. Although I had the run of the house and of the entire town, and all the money one could ever wish to spend, I became a prisoner inside my own mind. My imaginary world became my only safe haven, as reality was no longer kind to me.

I tried everything possible to block out the memory of that unforgettable night. On the other hand, I was lost without the memory, desperately needing some reference for my life. With little will to continue, I loaded one metaphorical bullet disguised as an overdose, into the chamber of my imaginary handgun, and every night I pulled the trigger in hopes of ending it all. I had so much money available, I could phone out for drugs like other kids called for a pizza. I called straight to the regional wholesalers, where purity was in abundance. Highly addictive mind-altering drugs became my closest companions.

Occasionally adults stopped by to see if I was still alive.

Their patronizing attitudes, though well-intentioned, made me run even further from authority. I was basically left to fend for myself. My sister came up from California for a while to help run the household, but she had friends all over town and I rarely saw her.

I finished out the school year in Aspen. My school was small, having less than a hundred students in each grade; most of my friends were seniors, mainly because they were the most reckless and irresponsible. Aspen High School on psychedelic drugs and other forms of intoxicants, we made home movies and enjoyed all weekend parties, ran around the Rocky Mountains seeking new adventures and dangerous ways to test our mortality. We played with jagged granite as though it was rubber, ran deadly rapids, and skied down the face of thousand-year old glaciers. Picture a bunch of teenagers running around stoned out of their minds and laughing their heads off.

Now, picture their outraged parents screaming and pointing at me, condemning me for ruining their dear innocent teenagers. And the real fun began when I sat down with these families at their dinner tables and put all of the responsibility for their children's behavior back on their shoulders. I accused them of trying to cover up their own failures and of an inability to reach their own children. And the next weekend we teenagers would be right back at it.

We followed each other down the rabbit hole. There was just one problem: helping to destroy their lives never seemed to make mine any better.

Because of my weak grades (I even failed a couple of classes), my father shipped me off down the valley to CRMS (Colorado Rocky Mountain School) for the summer in hopes I would pull up my grade average. That was the summer Neil Armstrong first stepped upon the moon.

I infested that student population with the ideas of a madman. I convinced half of the students to consume a very powerful psychedelic drug. While a large group of us went wild in Aspen watching an entertaining opera about the devil, the remainder stayed at the school and ended up on a climbing expedition with ropes and pitons and hammers, making their way up the walls and across the ceilings of the dormitory. Knowing I was to blame, the faculty took pity on me, and asked if I would be so kind as to have my father autograph their Uris novels.

Lee's frustration in handling a revolutionary became evident on a regular basis. Like clockwork, every afternoon at four, on the intercom I would hear, "Son, come over to my office."

Just by looking at his blood red eyes and angry expression, I realized that I was doomed to another lecture on my insensitivity. It reminded me of the dog that always bites and barks, only so that his master will pay attention to him. The beatings never bothered the dog and neither did my father's brutal lectures.

The conversations were not all one-sided. I held my ground and was as compassionate and respectful as possible. After several failed attempts to restore some kind of rational co-existence, Lee shipped me back to California like a caged animal or a damaged parcel.

***

Both of my parents eventually remarried. Mom married Frank, a great guy whom she met at a nudist colony. My father married a Bostonian two years younger than my sister; his new wife was a local Aspen photographer. Being in California was just what I needed to distance my life from the turmoil experienced during the previous year in Colorado.

I lived with my Mom and her new husband, Frank, in Santa Monica. He was always the voice of reason, yet he never patronized me. Having two of his own, Frank knew how to handle wild boys without loading them up with guilt and recrimination. Third in command at a large corporation, Frank was kind, thoughtful and patient to a fault. Besides my father and brother, Frank assumed the role of a caring mentor and role model, and I am a better person for having known him. He never raised his voice in anger at my mother, and offered her nothing less than enduring affection. They spent the remainder of their days loving one another. In her second marriage Betty settled for the best in Frank, however truth be told, she missed the bad boy, the conflict and passion that only Lee was willing to offer.

In Santa Monica, I entered the eleventh grade and immediately got expelled from Santa Monica High School for rebellious behavior and inciting riots; I led student protests against the Vietnam War. To avoid the war controversy the dean stated the reason for dismissal was long hair. I ended up at Palisades High School where my long hair wasn't such a problem, and the war protests continued as part of my extracurricular activities.

I even spent some of my free time in a tee-pee on a ranch in Malibu chewing peyote and raw opium and jamming with musical instruments. I played the drums, guitar and organ and I did not know any cords, and I could not keep a beat, and I could not sing, but we all had great times.

It was an era that I tested my own mortality on far too many occasions.

Luckily the lighter side of my character kept me alive despite my lust for oblivion. I continued to practice transcendental meditation. This evolved into practicing Hatha, Kundalini and Tantric yoga. All of these avenues towards self-realization ran parallel to my more destructive behavior.

In addition to my spiritual quest, I studied metaphysics. My metaphysician Jacques Honduras taught me how powerful the mind could be. We tapped into the energy that surrounds us like radio waves and I learned how to send and receive thoughts. The verdict of insanity is still out on that one. Jacques also honed my ability to hypnotize people, something I first learned from my brother, who learned it from his Spanish teacher, Professor Alamo, who was eventually banned from the school district for inappropriate behavior. I gave up this practice when I made my friend Eric think he was a goose so he wouldn't be afraid of going in the water. Unfortunately, I couldn't bring him out of it and Eric ended up in the hospital for days.

I believe my father had a hypnotic power over people. When he gave speeches, he drew the audience in. It wasn't so much the words as the way Lee projected them. So, in many ways I developed my own talents that would parallel those of my father, each of us choosing our own destiny to travel. Even though I lived a thousand miles away, I felt my father watching over me—if only from a distance—he continued to influence my every move.

***

Without a balance in my life, it would have ended long ago. The yoga and other non-toxic forms of self-realization became more important to me than all my years of formal education. These philosophical principles formed a solid foundation for me to stand on. Just as the hero is only as powerful as his adversary requires him to be, my darker nature grew in strength and determination in proportion to that of my nobler side. And at age seventeen the war for supremacy was well under way.

***

The three letters below were written around this time and best illustrate what was happening from my mother and father's points of view:

Letter from my mother :

Dear Lee,

I found a loaded gun, a couple of garbage bags full of pot, a flight bag full of pills, little bags of brown and white powder, rolling papers and a lot of money, thousands, mostly in large bills, all hidden in a corner of the basement. I took the gun, pills and powder and threw them in the trash. I'm not a bad mother – I left him one bag of pot – and if he wants the money back he'll have to ask me for it. Lee, it's the second time I found a loaded pistol in his things in the past few months. I can't deal with the artillery – I thought he got over that after seeing the psychiatrist when he was fourteen.

Two weeks ago – his best friend was thrown into Juvenile Hall for selling harmful drugs at a school dance, and his mother, Beverly Slate, told me in confidence that Mike is probably the ringleader. When Mike goes to work parking cars he rarely if ever comes home that night, sometimes he is gone for days at a time and when he comes back he goes straight to his room and locks the door. His laundry smells like pot and perfume. A friend of mine saw him at a swanky nightclub with a woman twice his age – and she was driving a Rolls.

I think he's a drug pusher just to be part of all the different crowds he hangs out with, but he makes real good money parking cars, so I don't understand why he needs all that money. He never buys anything for himself, that I know of, and always talks about how chasing after money screwed you up. His grades have slipped and some of the girls he dates are so high they can barely remember their own names. Mike's eyes are usually red so he must be high on something strong, or coming down from something worse. Thank God for small favors, at least he's not an alcoholic. He has that vegetarian diet and he is so skinny. I think he lives on air.

Somehow Mike is a good boy under all of his ruggedness and he seems to care about family and really wants to do well with school. He gets along great with his stepfather and he has this spiritual side that is really quite remarkable. Maybe we can send him off to private school where they can keep a close eye on him in a controlled environment? You know how he fights any idea of ours – I doubt he would leave his friends, especially his girlfriends.

All my best, Betty

My father's reply:

Dear Betty,

Thanks for the letter. I am appreciative of the response because communication between us in matters regarding the children is essential.

I talked with Mike on the phone yesterday and scolded him about having a gun. Who knows who Mike might have harmed with that gun, especially himself. That brown powder was heroin, the white cocaine, and he said they belonged to one of his girlfriends, Cynthia or Debbie I think... it's hard to keep track. I didn't say anything about the money or pot or pills... those are not as important issues, hopefully. I do understand the overall picture as being anything but palatable.

What I am concerned about is making certain we as parents are here for him and have never, nor will we ever desert him under any circumstances. What I propose is to broaden his outlook on life.

From what I've learned, St. Paul's is one of the finest prep schools anywhere with students from all over the world. This is an important matter for you to consider and I would like to see Mike go to St. Paul's for his senior year. I feel it would add to his feeling of wellbeing. Mainly, I think Mike will flourish in the atmosphere. He rejected the idea on the phone, so please try to reason with him. That is, if you agree sending him away might help. It is hard to believe our son is so confused.

I understand that the prospect of having Mike away from home is not pleasurable for you but, realistically speaking, he is growing up fast and needs to be in respectable company. We as parents must do what's best for him and we must do whatever is necessary to give him the finest possible education and a loving family to come home to.

Let me know your decision immediately as getting him into the school will take a bit of doing.

Love, Lee

My mother to her parents in Iowa:

Dear Mom and Dad,

Seems like time goes too fast and I'm not getting much done. Mark leaves in a few days for Aspen and then will go onto Boulder for the university year. Lee has been fussing about money, and after he promised Mark this and that, Lee is making more and more demands, and Mark's getting angrier and angrier with him. Mark gets so uptight and sensitive around Lee, and Mark always walks away abruptly and leaves Lee devastated. Mark is a fighter and I think he needs to stand his ground in order to be his own man, and not just the son of a famous writer. One day they will resolve their problems, they are both very smart and they both love each other very much.

I believe Mark is stalling, because of leaving here and also facing college and mostly the unknown with Lee. It shouldn't bother me anymore, but it still does – as long as it bothers the children – which it seems to. They now all have stomach spasms (instead of ulcers the doctor said) when they get tense or when their father gets angry with them, which is quite frequent. The boys take tranquilizers to stop hand tremors and both of them get very nervous speaking to crowds. Mike has that horrible stammer that just makes me want to cry.

I think both boys are smarter than their father and it drives him crazy sometimes trying to debate with their lack of unaligned patronage. I know Lee wants the boys to just love him as a father, but he forces them into constantly looking up to him as the public does. That is wrong and Lee knows it and he has suffered for years with the boys because of his ego. The sad part is that Lee loves them terribly and just doesn't know how to be a good father anymore – not like in the old days before he became such a big shot.

Lee wants to send Mike to a military school to finish out High School. Mike already rejected going to a very well respected prep school back east, stating he didn't want to be away from his friends out here. Lee is beside himself with Mike and is afraid, like me, that our little boy is, well, maybe making the wrong decisions in life.

Frank wants Mike to finish his senior year here and feels we can at least offer him a good family foundation. Whether or not he comes around is entirely up to him.

I think it's too late for military school. Maybe three years ago might have worked. Mike took the death of his stepmother just awful, he was so close to her, and I honestly think having him around a military environment and a bunch of guns isn't all that sound of an idea. Frank is generally right, having raised two older boys of his own. I think it would be much better for Mike to go to school here, at least till he finishes out High School.

I don't know – Mike's been shifted around plenty lately and taking care of himself most of the time. He's going up to Aspen in another week, and his Dad won't be in town. Mike is pretty upset that Dad is treating Mark so awful. Both boys love and need their father but Lee is playing Sugar Daddy to what's her name – the new girl. I think if Lee ever comes down hard on Mark, Mike will go after Lee and beat the tar out of him. Lee raised his boys tough and he'd better understand that discipline could backfire if he's not careful with what he says and the way he acts. Lee never grew up himself and is still trying to please his own father, so he should know better and just allow his own boys to love him the way they best see fit.

Mike can be quite the hoodlum at times... not his real respectable side. But we are working on it. Both boys are so sweet and likable when they want to be. Mike is a handsome fella and does have a lot of girlfriends always chasing after him – and he has this spiritual side that I think will one day take hold and steer him in the right direction, if he doesn't hurt himself first.

How can life be so confusing, Mom and Dad? I don't know why these boys make me worry so. I just love them to pieces and I know Lee does as well.

All my love, Betty

8

Running Away

In the summer of 1970 when I was seventeen, after completing the eleventh grade at Pacific Palisades High School, I drove up to Aspen in my Volkswagen van. Lee was now with his third wife, but they were out of town for the summer. My older brother Mark Jay was currently in Los Angeles visiting our mother, and planned to visit me in Aspen before heading to Boulder to attend the University of Colorado in the fall.

The main purpose of the trip would be to finalize my dealing career by delivering a footlocker full of hashish to an old acquaintance.

I had the run of Lee's house and one fine day I found myself looking for a book to read in his extensive library. While standing on a ladder and reaching to the top shelf, my hand came into contact with what would become my saving grace. By pure coincidence I found my Holy Grail, a significant work of literature that contained the spiritual teachings I had been searching for my entire life. *The Path of the Masters* by Dr. Julian Johnson laid out a practical scientific procedure on how to reach the ultimate reality, to reach inner realms so subtle that only pure consciousness could grasp these esoteric concepts.

The book changed my perspective on life, and offered me a method to connect with and confirm the existence of an individual soul. At age seventeen, I finally found a barometer to gauge the upcoming storms within my own mind.

While waiting for my brother Mark Jay to arrive in town I decided to take in the natural scenery and attempt a solo-climb to the top of a 14,000-foot mountain near Aspen named Cathedral Peak.

Three years before, at the age of fourteen, I attended a mountaineering survival school and learned climbing and survival techniques. My definition of a survival school is: "A place where wealthy people bet with the odds that natural selection will occur and nature will take care of their demon seed." Also: "That which doesn't accidentally take my child's life will only make him stronger."

Just the previous summer, one of the mountaineering students died while crossing a river and we would be faced with such dangers countless times. Were my parents giving me the opportunity to build my character and become a stronger person or were they giving me an easy way out? My father always boasted that facing death during World War II, in the Marine Corps, made a man out of him. From what I understood, he spent most of his time playing cards and writing letters home, and he saw little, if any, frontline action like the adventures he wrote about in *Battle Cry*. Funny thing, upon arrival at the survival school, none of the other mountaineering students knew that a student died the previous summer. Oddly enough, most of our parents were fully aware of the incident but somehow forgot to mention it to us.

Since surviving the survival school, I had climbed several of the tallest peaks in the Rocky Mountains. As far as climbing safety went, I was confidant and allowed my better judgment and climbing experience to make the hard decisions. This was my mark of bravery.

I faced certain death and challenged the odds with combat-tested confidence. A step in the wrong place, or trusting an unstable rock to hold your weight, would be your last mistake. The mountain peaks around Aspen have claimed the lives of far too many inexperienced and risk-taking climbers, and I didn't intend to end up as one of those statistics.

In early spring of 1969, just months after Margery died, two of my local school friends and I reached the summit of Pyramid Peak. We fearlessly climbed straight up walls of ice and frozen rock with strong psychedelic drugs running through our veins. We were so high, the solid granite rocks squeezed like sponges in our hands and our depth perception was so cosmically aligned we took impossible giant leaps and somehow connected with the calculated landing points. The constant adrenalin pumping though our hearts was so powerful that if we had wings it would have been simpler to fly to the top. That day we could have died at every step, but instead, we followed our intuition and were spared, not by any accomplishment of our own, but by some greater force in the universe that graciously watched over us. Although our early spring climb was considered foolish, threatened by constant avalanche danger, we were beaten to the top a few weeks earlier by a team of world-class climbers from Europe. But I don't think they were tripping.

***

Back to my 14,000-foot solo climb of Cathedral Peak. I parked my Volkswagen van as high as the road would take me (10,500 feet), then hiked another 2,000 feet to the timberline. Above the trees, the climb became much more difficult. Instead of attacking the mountain in all its merciless glory, I chose a ridge route. It was still considered a very dangerous climb. This was not a test of my climbing skills, and I had no grand purpose other than self-reflection and to enjoy the wonders of nature.

My knapsack held the very basic necessities, food and water, a sweater and a rainproof poncho. I forged ahead up the mountain ridge trail, higher and higher with each carefully calculated step, reaching for only the most secure handholds. After a few hours of relentless climbing, following the safest routes attainable, I finally made it to the top of the mountain.

Being a clear day the view was spectacular. I could see close to a hundred miles in any direction. I was standing on top of the world. Even though the route I chose did not require ropes and additional apparatus, anything could have happened. A solo climb is a marvel of accomplishment in itself. To take that risk, you have to trust in your own ability, have faith in your judgment.

No matter where I went in this world and no matter what I tried to accomplish, in the end, I only had myself to depend on. And to find the drive and inspiration within myself to make this solo climb not only proved to me that I was capable of traveling through life, but that I wanted to survive, at least for the time being.

My plan for that evening, was to consume some wonderfully cosmic magic mushrooms, actually several doses of a very rare and exotic variety only found in the rain forests of South America; in hopes of reaching the highest plateau of reality imaginable, much higher than the sober one I was currently experiencing. So much for enjoying nature with a clear head! I once again loaded up my metaphorical handgun and fired away at yet another attempt to overdose and turn out the lights.

Before long the sun fell into the horizon and an incredible display of a hundred shades of blending pastel colors encircled me. Like a laser lightshow, I witnessed amazing rainbows and glimmering shooting stars. The psychedelics made a single sparkler turn into a fireworks display.

***

As the colors faded and darkness arrived, I finally had two very profound revelations: I was still on top of the mountain—I had forgotten to go back down. The thin air rapidly grew colder. Since it was a beautiful starlit night, I dug a hole about eighteen inches deep in the loose shale rock and made an oval shaped bed to sleep in.

The loose shale on top of the mountain were once huge boulders, that over millions of years were weakened by wind and rain and blasted by lightning bolts into millions of pieces, somewhat like broken pieces of a ceramic container. The shards were scattered all over the mountaintop, in some places several feet thick. Not twenty feet away from where I made my bed in the shale was a fifteen-foot tall lightening rod, a safety precaution to draw lightening away from anyone who was stupid enough to be on the mountaintop during a storm.

The stars above me faded from view, which meant rain clouds were beginning to form in the area. To seek shelter from a rainstorm in the dark and risk falling would be as foolhardy as staying on top, both of which could cause an instant end of life experience. I ignored any potential danger, and put on my sweater, and covered my little oval bed in the shale with my waterproof poncho.

I heard thunder booming, and through a slit in the poncho I could see tremendous bolts of lightning crackling about a mile away. The strikes grew closer and closer. It began to rain. Before long, it was like a hurricane at sea and sheets of rain pounded onto my poncho. Bolts hit the nearby rod time and time again.

The thunder was so loud I covered my ears with my hands and still the noise level was so intense it almost burst my eardrums. And every time a lightning bolt struck the rod, it sent incredible amounts of diffused electrical energy directly into the loose shale. The rainwater all around conducted the electricity. The feeling was like sticking your entire body into a light socket; electrocution on a minor scale. It was like the sensation of a thousand bee stings and my body convulsed as though having a seizure. The electricity mixed with the surrounding groundwater sounded like sizzling water drops falling on a huge red-hot skillet.

Then, all of a sudden, one single gigantic bolt hit the rod. That one strike had the intensity of several of the previous ones combined. I pressed my hands against my ears. It was so bright I could see the mountaintop perfectly, even with my eyes closed. With that surge of electricity, my brain felt like it was going to explode. Then, my body went numb and the pain disappeared. That was the last I could remember before I passed out.

It became a night of dreams and memories...

I was eleven years old and surfing on my new board. For a while the waves were manageable and fun to ride. (My parents had been arguing the night before, and due to the emotional stress I had a severe psychosomatic breakdown in the middle of the night. Doctor Pobirs, the family doctor had to come out to our Malibu home at two in the morning to assure me that I wasn't dying.)

The waves began to grow in size and strength, so I decided to paddle outside past the unruly breakers. I needed to reach calmer waters to gain some kind of clarity in hopes this clarity would somehow ease the unavoidable stress I experienced from my parent's fighting.

After a while, I thought about paddling back to the beach, but a powerful riptide kept pushing everything off the shore. Huge swells continued to march my way and these transformed into magnificent waves, larger than any I had ever seen before. With every passing minute, I became more scared and confused.

The waves had grown to nearly twelve feet tall. Just one wave that size was like a wall of locomotives rushing at me. The waves were so large and so frequent that even if I had the strength and courage to paddle back to shore, the giant waves would likely break me in half.

I had visions of our family doctor staring at me and wondering why I did so many foolish things just to get attention from my parents. This was no different of a cry, than when I fell off my bike or out of a tree or accidentally cut myself, on purpose.

It was then a brilliant thought came across my mind; I'd just stay out in the water and never return to shore. I would no longer have to deal with my parents shouting at each other. I thought that I was the root of their problem, that I had the power to end all their trouble. So, I turned around and began to paddle my surfboard out to the open sea.

It was then I noticed a surfer paddling out from shore, fighting every inch of the way to get closer to me, risking his own life in an apparent rescue attempt. So I stopped paddling and waited for him to arrive. A few minutes later, the surfer had battled his way right through those giant waves. And like a guardian angel, the brave surfer eventually made it to my side.

I had never seen the man before, but he looked like a typical twenty-something tanned surfer with long dirty blond hair and a scrubby beard.

"Hi. I'm Sandy. Are you all right?" He smiled at me.

"I'm real nervous. Tried to get to shore but the riptide pushed me out, and the waves became too big to ride." I pointed at a swell that just passed by. "That one is nearly fifteen feet tall."

"The ocean is dangerous, even if there are no waves at all."

"The surf built up out of nowhere."

"I noticed you were paddling further out to sea. What's out there?"

"Searching for a way to solve all my problems," I said.

"Running away is not a solution. It only creates that many more problems for the people who love you." He paddled closer.

The giant swells continued to roll by, one right after another. Sandy and I kept going up and then down with the huge swells. Going back to the beach no longer seemed like an option.

Sandy turned to me and asked, "What's really bothering you?"

"My parents were fighting."

"So, you are trying to get their attention by coming out here in this huge surf. That does not seem very intelligent."

"I don't know what to think anymore."

"Maybe you just needed to come out here to think."

"Look, I'm not going to lie to you. I am pretty upset. I just feel like I'm in the way."

Sandy asked, "I didn't paddle out here to upset you." He carefully observed the waves for a minute. "It sounds like you want to go back to shore, but we can sit out here and talk for a while if you want."

I looked at the huge breakers. "I need to think. I'm not certain if I even want to go back home." I started crying.

Sandy stared at me like our family doctor. "Tell me what is really going on."

At this point I had everything to lose, but I had a clear choice. Honesty would be my only redemption. "My dad has been messing around with other women. At times I heard my father bragging about it to his friends. He goes on these long trips. Sometimes, I hear my mom crying in the other room. And then he would come home and say mean things to her. Nothing she did was right, and he made fun of her in hurtful ways. And she would start to cry, but he wouldn't stop and kept on cutting her down. He would say she was jealous of his success, and that she didn't have any friends. That she couldn't take care of the house, or us kids, or him, or even herself. Problem is, Dad really loves Mom and when he is finished yelling at her, she starts to pick on him and she yells too, saying what a horrible father he is, what a bad husband he is and that he thinks the world goes around him like he is God. She says he doesn't care about anyone as much as his career. She's angry because he won't let her be her own person, only the wife of an author, and she is tired of playing the role of a perfect wife. She tells him that she's glad when he goes out of town so she does not have to listen to his lies and anger. She is tired of living in hell and she misses the way he used to be before he was famous. When Dad is not around, she cries a lot, because it hurts her, because she loves him. When she stops yelling at him, she says how much she really loves him and how glamorous her life has been and how she lives for her family and husband, and that she is not proud of being less exciting than him, and she would rather work hard for his affection than be spoiled and not do anything around the house at all. And then Dad tells her that life is awfully hard and he chose a difficult career and without her love and understanding, he would have never made it this far. He says that there is no greater person in the world than the devoted wife of an author, and then they hug and kiss and go to sleep."

"Everyone has problems," Sandy said. "Your parents' problems are not your own. Look, kid." Sandy pointed at the beach. "Isn't that your mom and dad waving at us?"

When I glanced toward the shoreline, I became excited. "It looks like they see us!" Turning to Sandy, I asked, "How did you know they're my parents?"

"Fifteen years ago they would've been my parents." Sandy said. "Looks like they want you to come home. Go on. Wave back to them and see how they respond."

I stood up on my board and reached my arms way out and

signaled to them. My parents waved back with both hands held high in the air, and jumped up and down, all excited, as though I was winning a race.

Facing the warming sun, with eyes closed Sandy smiled and just sat on his surfboard. The huge swells continued to come towards us. He looked over at me and said, "You're very brave, to be out here in these waves. But when you get back to shore that is when you really need to show your bravery, in allowing your parents to live their own lives. Think about it, Mike."

"Wait," I wondered. "How did you know my name? Did my parents send you out here to rescue me? Are you some kind of a surfing shrink?"

"Who I am doesn't matter. The important thing is that you believe in yourself." A few moments later, Sandy pointed at an incredibly huge swell coming our way. "Are you ready to go home?"

I nodded and nervously replied, "That wave is as big as a house."

Sandy smiled. "The bigger the wave, the better chance we have to make it all the way to shore. The risk involved is worth the rewards, and the more you will prove to your parents that you want to be with them, that you need to be with them and that everything is going to be all right. And no matter what they decide to do with their lives, you have your own life to live."

"Thanks for... thanks for saving me." The problems at home seemed as huge and as uncontrollable as the large waves that were about to devour me. I had no idea where Sandy came from, but I appreciated having him around.

Sandy smiled at me. We started to paddle as fast as possible, heading directly towards shore. He yelled, "Keep paddling, follow my lead, and stand up when I do, and not a moment before!"

When Sandy stood up, I stood up as well, and we caught the giant wave. Sandy and I flew across that sheer wall of shimmering diamonds like proud warriors on golden platforms. Everything moved in slow motion. I looked toward the shoreline where my parents were waving and cheering.

And as we neared shore, the wave's wall of water closed out, and crashed down on the two of us with the force of a cement wall. Sandy dove headfirst into the water. The wave grabbed my surfboard and spit it out towards shore. I took a giant breath of air and closed my eyes. The water yanked me under and I was consumed by a giant mass of swirling water.

I managed to hold my breath, but the turbulent water was too powerful for me to deal with, and I helplessly flipped around like a doll in a washing machine.

It was then that someone very strong grabbed onto my arm. A few seconds later, my head made it to the surface and I gasped for air. I opened my eyes. With the look of welcomed relief and gratitude in his smile, my rescuer looked at me and asked, "Son... are you alright?"

Dad held me tightly, and after negotiating a couple more crashing waves we eventually made our way to the safety of shore.

When we got to the beach, Mom threw her arms around me. She cried with relief and squeezed out what air was left in me. Then Dad joined in and they both hugged me, and told me how much they loved me, and how glad they were that I made it safely home.

I stood up and looked all around, up and down the beach and in the water and out past the breaking waves. "Where's Sandy?" I asked my parents. "He paddled out to save me, and together we rode that giant wave."

Mom looked around, and then stared at me. "You were the only one out in the water."

I continued to look around in defense of my sanity. After a few moments I finally realized there never was anyone else.

Dad stared at me. "Son, tell me everything is going to be alright."

I hugged my father.

Mom asked, "Going out in that surf was foolish enough. Did you take that large wave on purpose, to hurt yourself?"

"No, Mom. I took that wave to come back to you."

I awoke sometime the next day on the top of Cathedral Peak...

I was suffering from several minor side effects from what seemed to be a combination of both the psychedelic mushrooms and the lightning strikes.

Everything I observed was in multiple patterns, like seeing the world through a kaleidoscope. You can imagine my surprise when I opened my eyes in the morning and saw dozens of much smaller suns all over the sky. It took me a few minutes to orient myself.

My hearing had been affected by the thunderclaps and there was a constant ringing in my ears. Everything seemed to have its own echo. I did not have to say anything more than a whisper and a multitude of minor echoes scattered in a multitude of directions.

But my newfound challenged sense perceptions didn't stop there. My sense of touch was almost completely gone. I was unable to feel anything. Even hitting my arm or stepping on my own foot offered no sensation at all. But I could still move.

And lastly, my sense of smell was gone.

My thought patterns seemed to be entirely normal. Hopefully the side effects from the electricity strikes and the psychedelic mushrooms would wear off in a matter of hours.

Getting off this mountaintop and back into town seemed to be the next order of the day. My brother would be arriving today from California and I needed to meet up with him by dinnertime. I was disoriented. It was cloudy and not seeing the position of the sun, I could not even estimate what time it was. All I knew was that it was imperative to get down the mountain before it got dark.

I left the top and forged my way down the ridge route. The numbness was an ironic relief. Finally, I wasn't feeling a thing, not about my irresponsible behavior nor my obligations to be a model student and the perfect son. I didn't feel a thing about unresolved issues, like Margery's death and my father's continued silence. I was probably safer on top of the mountain during a lightning strike than dealing with life at the base. I had finally gone over the edge, and now in losing my mind discovered a serenity that had long eluded my existence.

***

As I continued starring in this theater of the absurd, before long I was laughing and listening to a thousand echoes of my own laughter bouncing back at me. I bumped into rocks and I felt nothing. I lost my balance and tumbled head over heels, only to pick myself up again. I still felt no pain. I just continued on my way and continued to laugh.

Feeling somewhat invincible, I picked up the pace and began to move at a very rapid speed, taking giant leaps forward, and jumping and laughing. I tumbled and tumbled and just seemed to bounce off the ground as though my bones were pliable. In record time, far less than an hour, I approached the base of the mountain where my Volkswagen van was parked. I was still laughing and listening to my own echo.

Just as I arrived at my van, five climbers were about to make the very same climb. All of them just stood and looked at me like I was some kind of rare form of wildlife.

One of the expedition members grabbed my arm. "My God, you need medical attention." His voice echoed dozens of times.

"Why?" I asked.

The man looked like dozens of little men all drifting around in my sight and the climbing team resembled nearly a hundred, all of them floating in my honeycomb vision, and all of them looked at me in bewilderment.

He said, "Your face... and all your limbs... and your body is covered in blood... and your clothes are ripped to shreds."

"Really?" I looked at myself in the rearview mirror of my van. Although it was hard to see clearly, I did notice a lot of red. The climber was absolutely correct. However, though my clothes were shredded, it seemed as though most of the cuts and abrasions were minor.

I faced the climbers. "Actually I took a spill near the top of the mountain. See, most of the blood is dried up."

"We've been watching you with binoculars for forty minutes," a climber said. "You've been running down the ridge all the way from the top. You fell nearly a hundred times and tumbled a quarter of the way down. And we heard you laughing as you came closer. I think you must be in shock."

"I was on the mountaintop during the storm last night and dug a shelter in the shale and covered myself with my poncho. Just went to sleep and then the lightening woke me up. But other than a little echo in my hearing and a little visual impairment and very minor numbness, I'm perfectly fine."

"Why were you laughing?"

"I smoked a joint before heading down," I lied.

Smoking pot did not seem to bother the longhaired climber. "Why the hurry?"

"I didn't want to be late for dinner."

He looked at his watch. "It's seven o'clock."

"Shit, I'm late."

"It's seven in the morning." He asked, "What day is it?"

"The day after yesterday and the day before tomorrow." I smiled.

"Best have a doctor check you out."

***

They obviously didn't feel right about letting me wander off unattended, so the climbing team took time out of their day to test for any sprains and broken bones, washed and dressed all my cuts and abrasions, and wrapped up some of the heavily bruised areas with ace bandages. I thoroughly enjoyed watching their hundreds of tiny hands doing all the medical procedures. I still couldn't feel a thing. When they were finished, I thanked them and they went on their way up the mountain in plenty of time for them to make it back down before sunset.

***

Falling all the way down the mountain and surviving was nothing to be proud of. I understood being invincible was only a stroke of luck and nothing that I actually deserved. Nevertheless, being insane was a truly euphoric experience. I had finally reached the edge of existence and nothing could hurt me now. As long as I kept running, the past could never catch me. The only problem was, once I snapped out of my altered state, reality would be waiting to slap me senseless.

I got into my van. My vision was extremely unusual, but I made a judgment call and decided it was safe enough to head into town. I drove to my father's house cautiously. After showering, redressing some of the wounds and changing into clean clothes, I wrote a note to my brother. It said that I was going into town to pick up some groceries. Afterward, I'd come back and we would go out for dinner, pizza if that sounded all right with him. I left the note on the kitchen table.

Now, I felt very tired and more disoriented and confused than earlier, so before going into town I took a short nap on the living room couch.

***

The phone rang and woke me up. It was my father. At least, I thought it was my father's voice on the phone. My audio perception had grown worse, with so much echoing, it was very difficult for me to hear anything. Anyway, he wanted me to meet him at the Aspen airport. This certainly surprised me because I thought my father was out of town for the summer. According to him, he had been planning this for quite some time, a special father and son trip to Jerusalem.

Elated that Dad wanted to spend quality time with me, without hesitation I drove to the Aspen airport where I boarded a private jet with my father and we flew directly to Israel.

Arriving in Jerusalem, Lee and I climbed into an awaiting limousine. After a leisurely drive through the city, the chauffeured limousine parked and Dad and I walked to the top of Mount Zion. And there we stood at the highest point in Jerusalem and waited and waited...

And then, one by one, people from all walks of life and ethnic backgrounds began to assemble, all of them being led by their own children. Eventually the streams of people transformed into rivers, and then the rivers merged into a vast ocean of humanity. It reached in every direction, as far as the eye could see.

Once everyone assembled, a silence filled the air. Everyone turned in our direction and two million eyes were staring at the two of us.

I said to Dad, "They are waiting for you to say something."

"I've got jetlag, Son." Lee sat on a nearby rock. "It's your turn."

"What turn?"

"For a speech." Dad reached into a paper sack and then began to shell peanuts and toss them into his mouth.

"Is this like the time you threw me into the deep end of the pool to force me how to learn to swim?"

Lee shelled another peanut. "You were a quick learner that day."

"What makes you think I can give a speech? What about my stammer?" I looked out at the assembled crowd.

"You're my son. I have confidence in you."

"You always thought I was not as smart as Mark Jay."

"Both you boys are smart in your own ways."

"When you used to tell people your son was special and happy, I always thought you were making an excuse to others because I would never amount to anything. And special and happy was a polite way of saying I am simpleminded and an underachiever."

"You are special to me, Son. And there's nothing wrong with being happy. And try not to stammer. It's embarrassing." Lee continued to eat the peanuts.

Turning away from the frustration of either not being understood or not understanding, I focused my attention on all the children in the crowd. Their innocence and resolve inspired me to speak the first word. That word was *peace*. And then, I spoke the second and third words without a stammer, and those words were, *for all*.

My father listened intently, although he continued to shell and eat the peanuts. Welcome to my world. That was my father. When I needed him the most in life, he was playing with his nuts.

One child in the nearby crowd repeated my three words, *peace for all*. Ten yards away another child repeated the same three words, and then another child and another. And where language remained a barrier, those words were translated into different languages until the three words could be clearly understood, in every direction, and as fast as the words could travel:

Peace for all. In a perfect world those words should be all that is needed. We no longer wish to live in fear and hate and violence.

Hardships must be faced. We must stand together on common ground and have the patience to understand and accept our differences.

If great things are seldom achieved easily, let peace and freedom be the exception to that rule.

We all share a common responsibility. We must learn to move towards common goals that work for all of us.

Those who hate you cannot win, unless you hate them back. Never turn away from even the vilest heart, and have the courage to reach out as a true friend.

And if the fence of hate or a wall of mistrust separates us from being neighbors, tear them down.

We all deserve more than what yesterday had to offer. We have gathered for our very survival.

No one can change the past. Everyone deserves a future.

The loved ones we have lost can never be replaced. Think long and hard before you sacrifice any more.

Dirt is not worth the loss of a single life.

We are but one family, all joined together since the beginning of time. Today we come together to welcome peace.

In closing, look out into the crowd around you and spot a person who you once hated or disagreed with. And find the courage in your heart to humbly walk up to them and offer your hand in friendship.

Today we all made a difference. Life comes first... this is our chance to make peace last.

And when I had finished speaking to the crowd, Lee rose and stood by my side. We looked at the massive assembly that stood before us. Now that I had my father's approval, it had become the finest day of my life.

The echoes of the children's voices eventually faded and only the faint whisper of a summer's breeze filled the air. People turned to the sky and watched as a hundred glorious rainbows appeared out of nowhere.

"What a beautiful day. And you didn't stammer once," my father said.

***

I looked away for just one moment, but when I looked back again my father had disappeared. At a complete loss, I called out, "Dad! Where are you Dad?" I rubbed my eyes.

I heard a man call out to me from the nearby crowd. He said, "Dad is out of town!" The man's voice sounded familiar.

"Who are you?" I asked.

"The brother of a stoned idiot," the man called out.

Everyone in the massive crowd appeared to be staring directly at me, once again waiting for me to say something. I recognized the voice, but as I looked in his direction I could see dozens of images of my brother. "Mark?"

"It's dinnertime! Pizza—or whatever you want," he said. "Nice speech, fool. Too bad your words fell on deaf ears."

"They all seem happy." Everyone in the crowd smiled at me.

"You just brought lasting peace to rotting garbage."

I looked around at all the million people standing in front of me. "What garbage?"

Concerned as any brother should be, Mark said, "Mike, why don't you sit down and rest."

"Probably not a bad idea," I answered.

My brother just stood and stared at me. "Do you need help?"

"Just give me a couple of minutes."

I was tired and had sharp pains in my head. I became dizzy and my vision was blurry so I followed my brother's suggestion, and sat down on a nearby boulder and closed my eyes. A couple of minutes later, the ache in my head subsided and I slowly rose to my feet. I stood there, becoming more familiar with my surroundings. My hearing didn't echo and my eyesight was no longer fractured.

But I was shocked at what I really saw. I wasn't standing on top of Mount Zion in Jerusalem. I was standing on the top of a thirty-foot tall mountain of garbage at the Aspen city dump. And there weren't a million people in the crowd, there were only mounds and valleys of rancid trash as far as the eye could see. I could testify to that since my sense of smell had returned as well.

And then I realized, that when I was up in my father's house and the phone rang, it must have been Dad on the other end of the line, but since I only heard echoes, my father's voice must have triggered something in my mind and I slipped into an illusionary reality.

I remembered rushing to the phone when it rang and there was a surge of blood to my head and that intense surge also carried the effects of the hallucinogenic mushrooms that still remained in my bloodstream. Then, I drove my van to the City Dump, and during that drive, I imagined I was going to the airport and flying to Israel.

The limousine I had just arrived in from the airport with my imaginary father was not a limousine at all. It was an old junky rusty sedan with no windows and no tires that was rotting away at the base of the piles of garbage. I sat alone in the junked car thinking my father and I were driving through Jerusalem on the way up to Mount Zion.

It all made perfect sense to me now. And Mark Jay's voice triggered another chemical reaction that ultimately brought me back to reality. Who would have ever guessed my brother's voice was indeed the voice of reason. It was a fairly rough landing back into the realm of sanity. At least my best friend was there to greet me.

"Are you okay?" Mark Jay asked.

"Nothing a few slices of pizza couldn't cure."

"What are all those bandages on your face and arms from?"

"Spent last night on the top of Cathedral Peak. Got a little battered coming down the ridge trail." Unfortunately, along with the return of my senses came significant pain and discomfort from all the cuts, and abrasions, bruises, pulled muscles and ligaments I had experienced from tumbling down the mountain trail. "Do you have any aspirin?"

"In the car," Mark Jay replied.

9

Strangers

I slowly climbed down off of my imaginary Mount Zion, and my brother and I walked over to his car and he gave me some aspirin.

I asked, "How did you find me?"

"Found your note in the kitchen. It said you were at the grocery store, but I checked, and they said you never came by. So, I drove around looking for you."

"But I am five miles out of town. How did you figure I would be at the dump?"

My brother hesitated. "Dad told me that a week after Margery died, the deputies found you here at four in the morning in the backseat of a rusty junked car."

"That only explains that you knew I came here once, a long time ago. How did you assume I was here now?" I interrogated my brother.

"Your penmanship on the note." Mark Jay added, "It looked like first grade scribble. I knew you were out of your mind... and possibly crying out for help."

"Just out of my mind this time." I did not realize that my father told my brother that story. Still, there was probably very little that my brother and father did not share when it came to trying to understand me. They both cared about me and protected me whenever they could. Regrettably, I rejected their interference on more than a few occasions. Yet my father and brother shared keen perception, and a unique ability to outguess me under most normal circumstances.

I said, "Guess I spaced out the groceries."

"Outer space is closer." Mark Jay laughed and shook his head in disbelief. Yet again he had found me in a compromising situation and my older and wiser brother merely took it in stride. As usual he adapted to these situations and caused me the least amount of embarrassment and disgrace, and did not want to further humiliate me by hearing the real story of how I ended up in my confused condition speaking to mountains of garbage.

My brother did not know what the hell I had taken, if anything at all, nor did he usually want to know about the way I constantly toyed with mortality. He had no idea that I had just recently been shot through with enough electricity to temporarily rearrange my physiology. That would be my little secret, at least for now. Being my voice of reason, this time, I believed Mark Jay would eventually demand answers.

I had little if anything to hide from my brother. Other than to him, I have seldom, if ever, found the need to prove anything, to anyone in this world. Having to explain what was going on inside my mind to random inquisitors was an invasion of privacy and an assault on my free will. I would rather be looked upon as out of my mind than to give up the right to be an independent thinker. Facing down public scrutiny was not only an art form that my brother and I held dear; at times it was a necessity. The outside world continually tested us, matching us against our super hero father, only in the end to realize our father was no match for the two of us united. To vent our frustrations at one another, in front of total strangers, was our litmus test. That night, the pizza parlor would become our stage. If the strangers turned away and rejected our words, then it was a clear sign that we were no longer sincere and honest with each other.

***

Naturally my brother insisted we each drive home so I could take a shower, change my bandages and put on some fresh clothing. Mark Jay drove us into town to the local pizza parlor.

We entered the dimly lit family style pizzeria and took one of the centrally located red plastic veneer booths.

My brother immediately set the pace. "How often do you fucking flip out and turn into an absolute lunatic?"

Nearly every head in the restaurant turned to adjust the volume.

Not only had the evening's entertainment finally arrived, my brother and I were the designated headliners.

I smiled at the patrons. "Nice. Now everyone here knows I'm a psycho. No big deal. They'll get over it."

We didn't need to order. The waitress knew me, and I already ordered before we left home. She came over and delivered our sodas, then casually winked at me.

"What's with the wink?" My brother smirked.

I leaned forward and whispered, "She has an older sister visiting from college. You don't mind going on a double date with your stupid little brother. Don't worry, it's tomorrow."

Mark Jay whispered, "That explains you being hot for pizza."

"Hot runs in her family." I sipped on my drink.

"You treat your body like a laboratory experiment." Mark Jay dove back in.

"I feel much better now, thank you. And my mind is clear."

"That's because there is nothing in your brain left to destroy."

The pizza came and the waitress blew me a kiss and winked. "Seven. There's a spy flick at the Isis. What about..." She looked at my brother.

"He's in." I smiled at my conservative brother.

She walked away.

I took a bite. "This pizza couldn't taste better."

"The pizza is good, but Mike, your life is a crappy movie."

"Worry about your own crappy life. By the way, I had a great year parking cars, like you give a shit."

A greater percentage of the forty patrons listened in on our conversation.

"Is parking cars a cover for being a drug dealing gigolo?"

"I see you've been talking to Mom again."

Mark Jay glared at me. "Between just yesterday and today, how many times did you try to kill yourself? What in the hell were you doing on the top of a mountain all night? Did you get too stoned and forget to come down? That makes sense. Or was it more involved, were you confused, or trapped, or just plain too afraid to come down? And yes, I do give a shit."

"Okay, Doctor Pobirs," I said, using the name of our family doctor. He had always looked to the underlying source of the many accidents I had as a kid. "I messed up. On top of the mountain, I spaced out what time it was."

"What was that shit at the city dump really about? Why is everything you do a cry for help?"

"Tell me brother, how many thousands of Valium have you squeezed out of Mom over the past five years?" I asked.

"Now that I'm in college she sends me as many as I need. Keeps my hands from shaking—so, big fucking deal."

"Trust me, you are better off shaking, than being dependent on drugs. They don't cure your problem; they only mask your symptoms. What happens when those pills aren't enough?"

"I was about to ask you the same thing," my brother said.

"I appreciate your concern. But insanity fits me better than any sane suit." I winked at the waitress.

"What do you want out of life? Drugs and screwing?" Mark Jay took a huge bite of pizza.

I thought for a moment. "I need friendship more than the sex. Everyone needs to feel wanted. Quit attacking me. There is no mystery here. I don't know what I want. One week, I want to be a lawyer, then a doctor, then a director and back to being a lawyer."

I hadn't even finished high school. Mark Jay was entering his third year in college. Of course, my goals weren't as clearly defined as his.

"Mike, you can't survive doing one reckless act after another! And don't tell me the condition I found you in today was responsible behavior."

"You just caught me on a bad day."

"And you think that's just a coincidence? You fall down every day."

"Is this some kind of drug abuse lecture Mom put you up to?"

"We don't conspire against you. We conspire for you. But she's not the only one who cares." Mark added, "Don't be so aggressive with your bad habits."

I stared at Mark. "How many times have I caught you in one of your sophomoric beer busts, slurring as you crawled along the walls, and holding onto furniture to keep from crashing to the floor. I might not say it, but if you ever fell hard and hurt yourself—it would devastate me."

Mark looked at me. "I don't deny being human. But whatever I do doesn't give you an excuse to audition for the role of superman."

"Fair enough." I took a sip of soda. "You saw the real me today, but I cannot recall being that high ever before. You try going through life always wondering when, not if, but when, your parents are going to ship you off to an asylum."

"Quit giving them reasons! Sure, Mom and Dad are afraid of pushing you away, but I'm not." He tapped his finger on the table. "Mom told me she keeps finding loaded weapons hidden in your stuff. I thought you got over that back when you were fourteen."

The winking waitress brought over another refill of soda. "This should cool you off."

I faced my brother. "I'm done with dealing and done with guns."

"What was in the envelope you gave the cop?"

"Which cop?" I asked.

"There was more than one?" Mark Jay appeared really upset. "Last spring, when Mom and Frank were out of town. You threw that big party. I flew in from Colorado for a visit. The cops showed up and I thought everyone was going to jail. Then you slipped an envelope to one of the cops in the backyard. What was that about?"

I was on the spot and began to sweat. Except for the waitress, who blew me a kiss, everyone in the restaurant stared at me as though I was Al Capone. I had no reason to lie, so I answered, "The cop sold me a quarter pound of cocaine he stole from the evidence lockup. Yeah, add crooked cops to the list." I took a gulp of soda. "I'm not dealing anymore. I swear."

"Shit Mike!" Mark Jay's hand shook as he pointed at me. "This afternoon, after I found your sad excuse for a note in the kitchen, suspicious, I went in your room and found your nearly empty footlocker. Inside was over twenty thousand dollars. What else was in the fucking footlocker?"

"You don't have to tell me." I was embarrassed. "I wasn't lying about no more dealing... just had to take care of a small loose end."

Mark looked around the restaurant.

One lady in the next booth blurted out, "What was in the footlocker?"

"A fucking Israeli Uzi machine gun!" Mark Jay took a gulp of soda.

"I promised Mom and Dad I wouldn't have anything to do with revolvers or pistols, not ever." I smiled. "So I bought a machine gun."

"That makes perfect sense." Mark Jay beat his head onto the wooden table a couple of times.

"It was my last drug deal."

"What about the Uzi?"

"I'll throw it away."

A man in a nearby booth interrupted, "I'll take the Uzi."

"Look for it at the dump." Mark Jay turned to me. "What about the money?"

"Keep it. Burn it. Go to Vegas. Just leave me enough for gas and food till I get back to California."

"This time, I actually believe you." My brother smiled.

Everyone in the pizza parlor continued to stare at us. It was a small restaurant and we did not have to raise our voices to be heard.

***

"What's at the heart of it all? Why did you really run down that mountain? What are you running away from? Tell me something I don't know," Mark said.

"Fuck you, Mark! You know I can't talk about it." I sat and stared at him.

"It's all about her death. I know it's not easy to deal with. But you shouldn't blame yourself."

"I don't want to go there."

"Can we ever?"

"Not tonight!"

"Does that mean never?"

"You know I was there when she died. I should have told the truth. Now I owe Dad, he lied for me."

"If anything, he lied for himself." Mark Jay sneered.

I caught my breath. "Sucking you into my drama is not what a brother does."

After taking a sip of soda Mark Jay said, "Whom in the hell are you defending anymore? She's dead. Dad moved on. Why don't you?"

"I would tell you, if I thought it would resolve one single fucking thing."

"So I spend the rest of my life wondering how Margery died? I know you two were messing around. I found a couple of her little love notes to you." Mark Jay sat back in his seat and crossed his arms.

"What notes?"

"I was empting the trash from our rooms one day. A note fell out and I read it. So, I rifled through your trash and found a couple more."

"Did you show them to Dad?" I stared at him.

"I wouldn't do that." Uncrossing his arms, he took a sip of soda. "Okay. You screwed Margery and Dad didn't care." Mark stared at me.

"Fuck you!"

"Then it's the truth." He glared at me.

"No, it's a lie. Dad did care." I sat back and stared at my brother, shaking.

Mark Jay held my shoulder to calm me down.

I immediately shrugged away from his hand. "Ouch! Sorry... my shoulder hurts from falling."

"You need X-rays tomorrow," he said. "Just remember, if you ever want to talk about it, you know I'm here. I won't judge you."

I sighed. "It's more messed up than you could ever imagine. Consider yourself lucky not knowing. I don't want to lose your respect."

"What makes you think I ever respected you?" Mark laughed.

"Fuck you, too." I smiled.

"You go for a run almost every day. I've seen you. It is like someone is chasing you. No one has an absolutely clear conscience. Everyone has secrets."

I gently held my shoulder. "You have your private shit going on with Dad, and you've had the common sense to leave me out of what you thought I didn't need to hear."

Mark Jay lightened the mood. "Hey, talking to an imaginary Dad at the city dump is easier than talking to the real one. I'll have to try it sometime."

I cheered up a bit. "One day Dad will be old and harmless."

"Sometimes I hate him, but never too much not to love him." My brother smiled.

***

I excused myself and went to the restroom. I was grateful that my brother and I were being so open with each other. We hadn't cleared the air since he went off to college two years ago. Returning I found my soda was refilled.

I took a sip. "The truth is, I really don't understand Dad at all anymore. We don't really have a relationship. I don't know if he understands himself anymore."

"Do you think it's easy what Dad does? All that pressure would explode your brain. He's responsible for so many people. Putting up a front for the public, the fans, the angry mobs and the lawsuits, the to-do list is never ending."

"I wonder if he'd ever want to go back to the way things were," I said.

"He couldn't get away from it all if he tried. He has an entourage that feeds off his celebrity and financial success. It's too late for him to give up the responsibility, even though I think he was happier before he became famous."

"Dad must think I'm nothing more than a suicidal loser."

Mark looked around the room at everyone, all eyes focused on the two of us. "Margery's death nearly killed you. You can't keep reliving that night. It's true, I've talked to Dad about it, and on a gut level, I asked him what really happened. And Dad told me..." he hesitated.

Angered, I confronted. "What did he tell you?"

"What didn't he tell me?" Mark sat back in his seat. "I know more about that night than I led you to believe. But like Dad said, if all of us are going to move forward we cannot keep drowning ourselves in the past."

"How poetic," I laughed. "And how pathetic my brother and father must think of me."

"When's the first time you tried to end it all, after her suicide? Can you tell the truth, or will you find greater comfort in living a lie."

I looked straight at Mark. Tears formed in my eyes as I showed all my cards. "The deputies found me in the car at the dump after Margery died. They found an empty bottle of sleeping pills beside me. I took them all. But I'd built up such a high tolerance to the pills, they only made me sick, and I threw them up all over myself.

If anything, I should have choked on my own vomit." I continued to stare at my brother, so ashamed of my actions and who I'd become. "And when the deputies arrived, they took turns silently laughing at me, as I tried to talk my way out of being caught in such a state. I was so stoned I couldn't move, yet alone offer coherent phrases. I could see it in their eyes. The son of a famous author was reduced to nothing more than comic relief, a suicidal joke to amuse them on that cold wintery night. And from there it became a hobby, stepping over the line and defying death, an amateur high-wire act, coming to your town for one night only. And it didn't matter what I did, to do myself under, a hand always reached out to rescue me, usually in the form of my own conscience. I could have died a hundred times, but I came back over and over again to smear my honor with shame. I understand I have done wrong, to others and to myself. Covering up lies of the past, with a truth that comes far too late, isn't that a poorly played hand?

So here I am, telling you the truth, pleading with myself, convincing you that I had no control over my actions when my life has now become a feeble attempt to reconstruct what will forever remain broken. My true intent is scattered into a thousand unrecognizable pieces that no longer fit into what I envisioned life would be. I had a dream of my world being nothing less than wonderful, and look at me now, covered in cuts and bruises. Still, I deny my world is anything but wonderful. That only proves I'm afraid to see the world as it really is. The promises I made to myself all became lies, and the dreams became nightmares. And now I fear to sleep, but being awake terrifies me more."

Mark Jay reached over and held my arm. I looked up to see his eyes were watery.

He said, "What would we do if we lost you? It would be the saddest day of my life. No matter what any of us do, we are all affected, and everyone is a victim." Mark smiled. "Cheer up, if anything I spared you the lecture Dad was dying to give."

I wiped a tear from my eye. "I know Dad loves me, I just want him to like me again."

"Dad said the same thing about you." Mark Jay winked at me. "I was talking to him on the phone and he's been talking to his publisher about a research trip next year. I suggested that he takes you along and he agreed. That way, the two of you can spend some time together. I think that's what you both need. Don't think about it, just do it."

This was Mark's not so subtle way of being the best big brother a guy could ever have. He knew me better than I knew myself, and it was high time I trusted someone, and it seemed as though he was sitting right in front of me.

I said, "Her sister's name is Jenny."

"Thanks." My brother nodded his head.

As we walked towards the entrance my brother and I respectfully offered the patrons a smile. Some were moved while others appeared to be in shock. As though we had accomplished an unsurmountable feat, everyone within reach patted us on the back as we walked by. At the front we tried to pay our bill at the cash register, but the owner refused to take our money. Instead he opened the door, and with a wink and a smile he wished us a goodnight.

10

Vienna

In 1971, the fall after I graduated from high school, I accompanied my father on a forty-day research trip around the world. We would visit Austria, Turkey, Iran, Afghanistan, Pakistan, Australia and finally New Zealand. I was eighteen and he was forty-six. It was over a year since I last saw him. I met up with him and his third wife, Jill, in Vienna. Since she came into his life, I didn't have much of a relationship with him, other than through forced pleasantries on the phone.

Lee originally met Jill when he bought me a French Beaulieu movie camera, not long after Margery's death. Making movies was one of the few productive things I had an interest in. He had asked a close friend, a woman, who ran the local photography school if she knew anyone who could help me learn to use the camera. She recommended Jill, partly because of her photographic knowledge, but more so to fill the void in Lee's life. It turned out that she didn't know much about this kind of camera, but she managed to wing it. My father and Jill saw something in one another that filled the missing gaps in their lives, and it wasn't long before he added another trophy to his collection.

An extrovert, her strong personality complemented what he desperately needed at this point in his life and for the following two decades they shared a unique relationship. The essence of their union was profoundly real and saturated in the purest form of love. Working as a team, they reflected the highest quality of professionalism attaining goals that placed them in a class of their own. Ardent sports fans, they enjoyed watching football and other sports. They also loved skiing, tennis and other lively adult functions. Yet in a perfect world, we are only human and riddled with faults and even our best choices must endure the consequences of emotional frailty. Over the years I grew in understanding that she had been the best suited partner for Lee. Right off the pages of a steamy novel, their intimacy rivaled any I've ever known, but just as Icarus flew too close to the sun, the wings of their love lost their feathers as the wax melted from the heat of their passion and betrayal.

On this trip around the world, Jill would travel no further than Istanbul. Besides the obvious reason that it was not easy for a modern Western woman to travel in an undeveloped Muslim country, she was also recovering from serious surgery, the aftermath of a car accident. Since we were scheduled to travel through areas where it would be difficult to get medical attention, she planned on leaving our company and would tour Ireland with her sister. Her Ireland trip later inspired Lee to write *Trinity*.

Dad didn't need to keep Jill away from me—for obvious reasons. She was Margery's polar opposite. So, any fears Lee may have harbored concerning the past were vague at best. At times I wonder what he told her about the Margery triangle that not too long before existed, and then I realized the shame I brought my father was too great a burden for him to share with a new love in his life. Although it hurt me not to remember, my father's wisdom to let the memory of Margery rest in peace, at least as far as others were concerned—was a wise sacrifice to make.

As far as I was concerned, this trip was a fresh start for Dad and I. This would be our grand attempt at some form of reconciliation. We loved each other, but our problem was translating that love into action. My father needed to prove to himself that he could mentor his own son, and most of his past fears stemmed from an inability to deal with me on a daily basis. I desperately wanted a relationship with my father. I felt he genuinely cared about me and was determined to bring me back into his life. This trip would be the greatest challenge our relationship ever faced.

On the phone before the trip, my father and I agreed to make up for lost time and create a stronger bond with each other. Since the death of Margery, it was common knowledge I had become a rebel. My father thought exposing me to the real world would improve my outlook on life and expand my horizons. He always wished I would catch the bug for scholarly pursuits.

Despite his edict that we should never mention Margery, I hoped in the back of my mind that we could be honest with one another and finally talk about what had happened. Maybe Lee would be man enough to step up to the plate, but more than likely I would have to instigate that conversation.

Lee had recently published *QB VII*, and was pondering what book to write next. He had a basic idea for a storyline but was in search of the perfect settings. Lee had unique access and, with the help of his publisher, doors were opened that had been sealed for decades.

We traveled with experienced guides, religious scholars, sociologists, and anthropologists. My father, experienced in photography, gathered research data, while I added motion picture footage and worked as his assistant. Thus, I contributed more than just being a casual traveling companion and a bewildered adolescent.

I was a vegetarian so in case there wasn't anything I could eat, I carried a daypack that contained dried fruit, nuts, and canned juice to supplement my meals. Whenever language became a barrier, I would walk right back into the kitchen and point to what I could or could not eat. Mostly, I kept my diet simple and never complained.

Welcome to Vienna in the cold days of autumn. Almost everyone wore long trench coats, hats, and scarves that perfectly matched their drab personalities. I constantly looked for at least one person to smile. Maybe my expectations were too high, just as I continually searched my father's expressions trying to locate a smile heading my direction. However, what I saw in the local population was probably just my interpretation of what was actually reflected from within the vast wasteland of my own disillusionment.

We stayed at the Imperial Hotel in the center of town. It was exquisite, comfortable and displayed a serene view of the park; my room was lavishly decorated with antiques.

Our balding Austrian guide, Helmut, wore a suit and tie. The thirty-something bullish gentleman displayed a crazed aggressive sense of wellbeing. His impatient attitude proved to be a constant threat to my father's state of mind. The instant we met Helmut, Dad whispered in my ear that Helmut was not to be trusted, that his father was probably a former Nazi concentration camp guard. Helmut might have been insensitive, but I doubt he was a closet Nazi. Unlike my father, I harbor no ill will towards anyone. I have a forgiving nature and consider all of us struggling souls. If one learns from their mistakes and evolves into a better person, how can we rightfully condemn their current actions?

Probably the most docile tour guide the prestigious hotel had to offer, all Helmut wanted was to make a decent living. You can be assured Dad was not the first outspoken Jew that Helmut led through Austria. Lee's intolerance of our guide only added to the Vienna tension. In Austria, at the time, it was illegal to honk your horn. The alternative was to rev your engine and Helmut acted like a racehorse chomping at the bit. At times it became so claustrophobic in the car, I had to roll down the window just to refresh the atmosphere.

An impassioned casualty of the war, my father had experienced hate and intolerance on a level I might never fully understand. Although his wisdom is clear, at times his anger took hold and ruled the day. Passing judgement on another works both ways. My father surely hurt Helmut's feelings in displaying his own form of intolerance. Hate and intolerance stops with the individual, otherwise the cycle will continue to future generations. Best sleep with one eye open, for the beast is within all of us and the nature of the beast will never die.

***

One day our trusty guide Helmut, my father, Jill, and I took a trip up north, into the woods a couple of hours from the city limits.

We drove deep into the forest and down a very long private road until we arrived at a very large villa flanked by a couple of smaller adjoining buildings.

This was a halfway house, a place to 'screen' Soviet Jews immigrating to Israel from various communist countries. Funded and operated by the Israeli government, the facility received Jewish immigrants who were in transit to Israel. They were fleeing any number of Soviet block countries. The greater percentage came from Russia and the Ukraine.

The compound's main purpose was to verify identification and interview the immigrants so as to weed out any Soviet Government spies who were intending to gather information on the resettlement network and the Israeli government. From what I understood, this was only one of several processing centers and everyone entering Israel was scrutinized. Though the most sophisticated procedures were implemented, counterintelligence agents still slipped into Israel.

In many cases, parts of extended families were allowed by the Soviet government to 'conveniently' leave the country. This raised flags of suspicion. Under threat that family members who remained in the Soviet Union would be subjected to imprisonment and physical harm, some of the émigrés were pressured to spy on Israel. Whatever the case, any person who compromised the overall safety and security of Israel was turned away at this villa.

During the tour of the facility we talked with several Israelis as well as with a number of the people waiting to leave for Israel. A plainly dressed woman in her mid-forties kept staring at my father. It seemed as though she recognized him, but could not quite place where she had seen him before. After a few minutes, she overheard my father's name and practically fainted. After regaining her composure, the woman approached one of the translators and asked for a brief audience with my father. She paced around in circles and muttered phrases to herself. Obviously excited, the blushing woman touched her heart with both hands.

Our translator talked with the woman and told us that she came from Kiev. She had read *Exodus* twelve years ago, two years after it was first published. The book was banned in the Soviet Union. The safest way to read it was one chapter at a time, passed on from person to person, in secrecy. It was seldom, if ever, read in its complete original form. Instead, it was transcribed by hand in the different local dialects and each chapter was carefully passed on from one person to the next. That way no one person could be caught with the entire book. Possession of the book carried a minimum sentence of three years in a harsh Siberian prison.

This woman had translated and hand copied several entire duplicates of the book. Then, she passed those chapters, one by one, to Jews and sympathetic Soviets over the next twelve years. This one task consumed her every spare hour over all of those years. The woman who stood before us was only one of many who translated my father's books. Even under the constant threat of imprisonment, these people would not surrender a cause so dear to their hearts. The dream of immigrating to Israel gave thousands of people a reason to live. For Soviet Jews *Exodus* became the most popular message of their time and most Soviet Jews of that era referred to it simply as 'the book.'

Back in the days of the Soviet Union it was illegal to be aligned with any religion. Yet, the Jews remained defiant and secretly continued to follow traditions and religious practices. The Jewish faith existed only in the shadows. Jews had always been guardians of the written word, but what they now lacked were books filled with hope and inspiration. Lee's Jewish father and uncles migrated from Russia and Poland—he understood the persecution they had endured. When *Exodus* and *Mila 18* arrived in the Soviet Union, my father's words answered their prayers.

My dad has a photograph of Golda Meir speaking in Moscow, during one of his visits while doing research for the book *Armageddon*. It was meant to be a small venue, but thousands of Jews came out of hiding and filled the surrounding area in defiance of the Soviet oppression. Until then, no one had any idea of how many Jews survived the decades of Communist rule. Her speech echoed through other countries and on that day, Jews all over the world came out of their homes and stood together, no longer afraid to be recognized.

***

As this woman in the woods outside of Vienna came face to face with the person who first inspired her to follow her dream of freedom, she was so emotionally overwhelmed that, after she hugged my father and thanked him, she broke down in tears, tears of joy. We were touched and felt no shame in showing our emotions. My father was brimming with pride at her warmth and gratitude. It was the first time I truly understood the power of the written word.

Dad understood how much the brief meeting meant to her. For him, it was the pinnacle of his career. Throughout my father's life, most people loved his work, but there were always a few who remained critical, and since that day in the Vienna Woods, Lee's pride of accomplishment would never have to be justified to anyone again. It was as though this woman handed my father the Nobel Prize, an honor he would have gladly accepted. The privilege to witness this event was something I have always treasured.

One day during our stay in Vienna, Helmut, Lee, Jill, and I made our way up north from the city. It would be one of the darkest days of my life.

After a two-hour drive north of Vienna, we arrived at a World War II monument. Dad wanted me to experience an Austrian Nazi prison work camp known as Mauthausen.

The moment we walked through the front gate of the labor camp we were transported back in time to a nightmare that had occurred just over two decades ago. When I first arrived at the labor camp I didn't know why anyone would maintain such a place as a monument. By the time I left, I fully understood why it must remain for all times as a memorial to the people who died there.

Inside the camp was a small museum that contained artifacts and many enlarged photographs. Most of them were taken during the liberation at the end of the war. Some depicted entire rooms stacked to the ceiling with eyeglasses. There were pictures of emaciated prisoners barely alive in their sleeping quarters; their skeletal figures were literally skin and bones. Stuffed into overcrowded rooms in inhumane living conditions, starved and frozen, these were the lucky ones compared to those who had suffered further.

Since that day I've visited many such museums and monuments. Talking with Holocaust survivors I listened to memories of events that would haunt them for the remainder of their lives. I commend their bravery for sharing those recollections with the world. Some things should never be forgotten—no matter how gruesome and horrid—lest we become complacent and forget. Gaining second hand knowledge through photos and personal accounts, I understood that Jews, Gypsies and others marked for death, were taken from their homes and packed into trains, traveling for days without food or water, transported to death camps, and upon arrival were stripped naked and marched into gas chambers. I've seen photos of trucks disguised as medical transports, packed with Jews and others, where the tailpipe of the vehicle went directly back into where the prisoners were kept, and then driven directly to mass graves or crematoriums.

The camp's main objective was to remove large stones from a quarry. They called it 'extermination through labor,' where prisoners were literally worked to death and if they did not die at the labor camp and were no longer able to work, they were sent to a nearby death camp. If you survived starvation and the nearly two hundred steps leading out of the quarry, you were still subjected to hideous medical experiments, humilation, rape, torture and other unthinkable acts ending in murder. These atrocities were daily occurrences over the several years the camp remained in operation. When Heinrich Himmler visited the camp, for his amusement the S.S. threw a thousand Dutch Jews off the 165-ft quarry cliffs to a certain death.

Walking through the labor camp, all of my senses came to life. As a whipping breeze took hold of the dust, I could smell the dried sweat and tears from the tortured prisoners. More blood had fallen here than rain. The tainted air filled my lungs with every breath and made me cry. I could hear faint echoes from a past era. These echoes of the past were now trapped inside my memory.

Having visited several such facilities throughout Europe, I doubt that Lee needed a refresher course on the insane, compassionless and cruel nature of humanity. This was a place my father did not want to visit—it was a place he needed to visit. One of his main goals in bringing me along on this trip was to expose me to the hardships and suffering outside of my bubble and awaken my conscience.

As for my father, having visited many death camps, and after interviewing hundreds and meeting thousands of Holocaust survivors, what he absorbed that day only strengthened his resolve to honor the fallen.

On my father's side of the family several relatives were lost to the Holocaust. Regrettably, too many perished at the hands of pure evil. For centuries my Jewish ancestors endured intolerance. Like Simon Wiesenthal, my father had never been afraid to point his finger at the injustice and the inhumanity of mankind. Lee dedicated his life to helping those still living, and in honoring the dead. His contributions will stand the test of time.

That day in the Austrian countryside, everywhere you turned there were echoes of death and suffering. A bloodstained granite wall peppered with bullet marks was just one of the many locations where prisoners were tortured and executed. I had seen my father looking at that wall, with tears streaming from his eyes. This was his private moment, vowing once again to his ancestors that he'd fight until his last breath to avenge these atrocities, and do everything in his power to be the voice of reason where there was none. I watched, as a great man didn't hold back his tears. Not afraid to show his emotions, he looked at me and smiled, as he saw my tears. The connection we shared would never be forgotten. It was a great moment for him, as he had finally reached me. And knowing my father genuinely cared about me, was the best feeling I can remember. This was the humanitarian who mentored me. This was how he shaped me in his own image and, for once, I was humbled. I felt truly grateful, and honored to be his son.

***

Helmut kept a low profile during the tour and wisely stayed in the shadows. There was no way he could have avoided the overflow of grief mixed with animosity. By the end of the day he had earned his wages the hard way.

When our tour ended, we drove back to Vienna. Few words were spoken. Returning to the hotel, I excused myself from attending dinner and went directly to my room.

I remember lying in bed and drifting off to sleep. After a few minutes, I woke up screaming and covered in sweat, with my heart pounding. I had dreamt that I was a prisoner in a death camp. In the nightmare, the experience seemed to last for several hours, when in reality it was only a short while. Terrified, as memories of Mauthausen haunted me, I huddled in a reading chair and prayed for the light of dawn. I was one of the lucky ones. I had survived my visit to the death camp. And with the morning sun my fear was gone, replaced with compassion for those who suffered and a firm resolve to never forget what had transpired.

11

Afghanistan Banana Stand

In Istanbul, Lee had an opportunity to spend some time with his wife before they parted company for a month. Dad's publisher got us the best suite at one of the international hotels and we had the entire top floor. There, my father and I smoked Turkish hashish that our guide purchased.

Although we went sightseeing during the day, my father spent most of the time enjoying the suite. I spent most of my time in local nightclubs with our guide and his mistress. It was the month of Ramadan and Muslims fasted during the day but the nightlife was nonstop and afforded me every opportunity to sow my own wild oats as the guide's mistress had a younger sister who took a fancy to me.

***

I tried to smuggle a few grams of hashish out of the Istanbul airport. I thought it harmless, considering the small amount was only for personal consumption. What I did not take into consideration was the volume of smuggling at the airport. This was the world of the movie *Midnight Express*. Swarming plain-clothed policemen roamed around looking for idiots like me. I began to sweat, and they must have noticed my nervousness. After a race to the bathroom, I got into a stall, and flushed the contraband. The relief on my face, as I exited the restroom, must have convinced the undercover officers that there was no longer any reason to detain me.

***

We finally boarded the jetliner and headed off towards our next stop in Tehran, Iran. We had front row seats in the First Class compartment. Considering I didn't get much sleep in Istanbul, I took a nap as soon as we sat down, and immediately fell into a deep sleep.

"Son, wake up!"

"Dad? Where am I... Oh, the jet... What's up?"

After downing a miniature bottle of vodka and taking a deep breath, my father sat back in his seat and anxiously informed me, "Kiss your ass goodbye. The captain just made an announcement. One of the four jet engines failed and the plane needs to make an emergency landing in Syria. They will drag us off the plane feet first and no one will ever hear from us again! Who knows what the hell they will do to us? We'll never get out of this alive! God damn it, I knew we should have flown a different route!"

"Calm down, Dad," I said, though my heart had just about stopped. Back in Vienna, Lee had mentioned that we might consider taking another route from Istanbul so we wouldn't be flying over any Arab countries that had it in for Lee.

Everyone in the First Class cabin was privy to Lee's panic attack. I reached up and pushed the call button for the flight attendant.

"They will probably start by cutting off my pecker! We've got to think of something, fast," Dad said.

"Don't get all freaked out, Dad. The pilot will help us. You'll see. And quit thinking about your penis."

The stewardess came by and cleared the call button.

"I've got to talk to the pilot! This is an emergency! But first can you pour me two of those vodka miniatures, in a large glass, with just a smidge of vermouth... thank you, Sweetheart." He winked at her.

Ever so swiftly, the stewardess returned with Dad's drink, and then walked to the flight cabin, and moments later she returned with the captain. Back in those days the flight cabins were seldom, if ever, locked and the flight crew often ventured back into the plane to stretch their legs and talk with the passengers.

Having already downed the vodka in seconds flat, my father ordered another large glass of vodka. At least the alcohol seemed to be relaxing him a little.

The pilot leaned over us. "Good evening, Sir. We are experiencing a few minor problems with the #3 engine, and had to shut her down. The stewardess said you were overly concerned about our unscheduled layover in Syria. I hope this isn't a problem for you."

"Are you fucking nuts? The Syrians will lock me in a dungeon and throw away the key."

"I assure you the Syrians will be perfect hosts during our brief layover. Everything will be just fine. We have a relief jet flying in from Istanbul. It will arrive in Syria in about three hours. Unfortunately, all passengers landing on Syrian soil are required by the Syrian Government to go through immigration passport checks. Naturally, we'll have to wait in the concourse immigration area for the relief flight to arrive. Then we'll be on our way. I apologize for any inconvenience," the pilot said.

"Are you certain we only have a failed engine? Is there something you are not telling us?" Dad asked.

"Just a minor malfunction. According to safety regulations, we are required to shut down the engine and land as soon as possible."

"Who is flying the plane now?" I asked.

"Auto pilot. My co-pilot got into the booze again, so I told him to take a nap and sleep it off."

"With any luck the plane will crash and we won't have to worry about being tortured," I said.

The pilot ignored me and just stood there and smiled at the other passengers. By this time almost everyone in the First Class cabin was listening in.

Lee gulped down another tall double vodka then smiled at the stewardess as he handed her the glass. "Sweet Lips, just one more double in a tall glass—and go easy on the vermouth."

Dad calmly informed the pilot: "I am Leon Uris. This is my son, and if this plane lands on Syrian soil, and they find out we are on board, the Syrian Government will declare a national holiday in honor of my capture."

I turned to the pilot. "Can't you see my father is upset?"

"I love you, Son, shut up." Dad was pretty drunk by then.

The pilot interrupted, "Mr. Uris. This is quite an honor. Wait till my wife and daughter and mother and Uncle Simon and Aunt Sheila hear about this. Why, strange as it might seem, I just happen to have a copy of *Mila 18* in the flight cabin. It was a marvelous story."

Though my father's books were bestsellers, I thought it was weird that the pilot had a copy of *Mila 18* handy. Something strange was going on, but I wasn't sure what it was.

"I'd be happy to autograph it for you, kind Sir, Mister Pilot, Sir," Dad said, with a slur.

"I'd be happier if we weren't landing in Syria," I said.

"We could land in the Soviet Union," the pilot offered.

"No!" a passenger blurted out. "They would throw me and my wife into a gulag. We escaped the Soviet Union, just last month!" He then pointed back to economy class. "Along with my daughter and my son and my mother-in-law and my father-in-law and my nephew and his wife, and we have two goats in cargo. My goats, I love them. Absolutely no! We do not land in the Soviet Union!"

The pilot whispered to me, "I hate this route. Damn refugees."

"I hate the commies," Dad said. "Onward to... where were we going? Oh, right, my son and I have an appointment—onward to destiny!" He pointed his finger in the air.

The pilot turned to my father. "Let me get that book before we land in Syria." He headed back to the cabin.

The stewardess returned with yet another tall vodka.

She leaned in over him, pressing her breasts against his face. "Why, aren't you the most handsome man I've ever served?"

"That's me, baby—handsome as hell," slurred Dad.

Ignoring her advances, I asked the stewardess, "Can I please have a Swiss cheese sandwich with mustard and potato chips, and a Coke?"

She winked at me. "Only if you promise to smile."

I took Dad's glass when he wasn't looking and handed it to the stewardess, then pointed at Dad and whispered, "I don't think he'd know if you served him watered-down vodka at this point." Then, in a normal voice, I said, "Can you be a love and freshen this up for my father?" I winked at her.

She returned in a minute with his drink.

Lee asked her, "Will you marry me? What is your name?"

"Sylvia. And yes, if the Syrians don't detain you I might consider your proposal. But aren't you already married?"

My father slurred, "We're over Syria, even though I'm Jewish, can't I have a harem?"

I laughed. Dad could be the charmer, even though he was about to drink himself under the foldout table.

He added, "Sylvia, I'm looking forward to spending the rest of my life with you." Dad winked at her.

She giggled. "How delightful. I can hardly wait for our nuptials." She turned and walked away.

"Dad. I'm worried about you. We're about to be abducted by the Syrians, and you are having your own little party."

***

The pilot returned with his copy of *Mila 18*. He handed the book and a pen to my father. "Could you make it out... to Constance and Phillip and Penelope, with all my love and admiration, you are the sweetest family I have ever known."

Dad spoke as he wrote, "Dear Phillip... you are the most wonderful pilot I have ever known and I will always be your very dearest friend. All my love and fondest admiration to you and your lovely ladies... Constance and Penelope... the sweetest family ever... till we meet again." Dad looked at the pilot. "Are you Jewish?"

"My wife is," he answered.

"Very well then. Yours very sincerely and shalom, Leon Uris." Dad smiled as he handed the pilot the book.

The pilot looked at Dad's note. "Thank you, Mr. Uris."

I gently banged my head against the window a few times to see if I was dreaming.

Dad glanced over at me. "Something wrong?"

"Just thinking," I said. Dad was such a good sport signing his autograph before it was all over. It may not have been his finest dedication, but it would certainly be his last.

***

A man stood up and walked down the aisle towards us. He was in his late sixties and distinguished looking. He wore an expensive tailored suit and walked directly up to Dad. The pilot and Dad stopped talking and faced the man, who looked like he might be an Arab.

In a firm voice he said, "So you are the Jew who wrote *Exodus*."

Dad stood up from his seat and faced the man. Still inebriated, he whimsically pointed his finger in the air. "I am that Jew!"

"I am a Muslim Turkish diplomat on a special envoy bringing a greeting to the Shah of Iran. I am married to a Jew. I am to meet my wife in Tehran tomorrow for a very special day."

"And what brings you to this fair aisle?"

The man reached into his coat pocket and pulled out a greeting card and a pen. "It is my wife's birthday tomorrow. *Exodus* is her favorite book. She loved the Kitty character so much she named our daughter after her."

Dad smiled and reached for the card and pen. "What is your lovely wife's name?"

One by one, more people, with cocktails in hand, approached and casually waited for an autograph. Some of the passengers just wanted to stretch their legs and offered their kind respects to Dad for being such a gentleman in the midst of impending doom. My father had his own special way of parting the Red Sea and everyone around him basked in the afterglow of his celebrity.

After all the signings, Dad started singing Sinatra songs to the First Class passengers, and even did a couple of duets with the stewardess. Even though he was drunk, he sang like he was sober. Everyone clapped, asking for more entertainment. It was a casual cocktail party in the sky.

Where in the world could you find a man hosting a party before his own execution? Welcome to the never-ending theater that orbited around my father. Wherever Lee was, he wanted to be the star.

***

I slipped out of my seat and cornered the pilot, who was not even flying the broken plane. He was talking with one of the passengers and drinking a cup of coffee. We sat down in a couple of empty seats. I took my butter knife and stuck it up to his ribs, right under his heart and whispered, "We are going to slowly stand up and go to the flight cabin and you are going to fly this fucking plane to Tehran." I lowered my voice so I would sound as authoritative as possible. "Is that fucking clear, Phillip?"

The pilot whispered, "Nice voice. You sing opera?"

This was insane.

Before I could say anything more, the pilot yelled over to Lee. "Leon! Your son finally made a move. Knife in the ribs, I win the pool! That's two hundred bucks."

I lowered the knife. "What?"

The pilot turned to me and explained that the whole thing was a hoax. No announcement of an emergency landing over the loudspeakers was ever made. When I was asleep at the beginning of the flight, Lee, the pilot and the other first class passengers decided to stage this entire melodrama.

I shook my head. "Nice performance. I should have seen this coming." I should have realized that my father was overacting, but he dove so deeply into his character I fell for his every word.

"The hardest part of the entire charade was not to laugh in your face. Your father was the mastermind."

"But he's so drunk."

"It was only water, not vodka." The pilot patted me on the shoulder, and then headed off towards the flight cabin.

This was my reality, where there was no difference between truth and fiction. Caught up in the moment, and everyone acted their parts so well, I never doubted the play. Blushing from embarrassment, I walked past everyone and returned to my seat beside Dad.

My father leaned over to me and said in a perfectly sober voice, "You risked your life to save me."

"I was bored. All the inflight magazines were mostly in foreign languages."

"I love you, Son." Dad smiled. "Got you good."

I smiled. "Pretty slick. But, when you dropped character and sang the Sinatra numbers without slurring, I had a feeling something was off."

"It would be a sin to mock Sinatra." Dad stood up and addressed the cabin. "He's a good sport! Thank you all!"

Everyone clapped and laughed. I turned and looked at them, then looked back at Lee. Up until this point in the trip, he hadn't been paying much attention to me. Jill had been there. But now, he'd taken the time to plan this elaborate practical joke. I was back in his good graces. He trusted me to be a good sport. Though the joke was on me, I was not humiliated; I was happy.

Still, revenge would be mine; if Dad wanted to play mind games and challenge my patience by dueling words of deception, then I was up for the challenge. What Dad didn't know was that I spent my entire life watching the master at work and at play, and it was time for me to show him that I could control the board.

***

During our ten-day research tour of Afghanistan, we scoured the countryside interviewing people who were born there, just visiting, or temporarily working in the country. Besides the odd characters who constantly crossed our path—the interviews and information gathering included U. S. State Department and Soviet personnel, the Afghan government and military, agricultural advisors, engineers, socio-economic scholars, religious leaders, and medical personnel.

Our guide, translator, and local confidant, forty-year old Professor Kakar, headed the anthropology department at the University of Kabul. He wore glasses and the same drab suit and tie every day. An influential yet very humble man, Kakar probably knew more about Afghanistan and its people than the past several Afghan presidents combined.

An experienced thirty-year old guide drove us everywhere in

his combat tested Range Rover. Scar-faced, tall and skinny Abdul wore a baggy white cotton outfit with a brown jacket. He always carried concealed weapons on his person and in his vehicle. He worked out of a privately owned Soviet nightclub and smuggler's den in Kabul. One of the best guides and bodyguards the country had to offer, Abdul was highly respected and gained us safe passage through places where tourists and even the U.S. State Department dared not go.

***

Let me explain a little about Afghanistan back in 1971. A police officer in Kabul earned the equivalent of about eighty cents a month with no benefits. An enlisted man in the army made ten cents a month along with room and board. Most commodities and services were bartered. Currency carried little value and was seldom used.

A merchant would travel one or two hundred miles with a camel, horse or a donkey loaded up with twigs and branches to be used to mix with clay to make bricks for building. The main source of cooking and heating fuel was animal dung, such as from the water buffalo. In the lower valleys, where all the larger cities and towns were situated the women did their laundry by hand in barely flowing muddy rivers.

Some of the world's most beautiful rugs and fabrics came from this region, and in almost all of the villages, you could find women weaving colorful silk and cotton tapestries from naturally dyed yarns. They wove garments and woollen rugs on handlooms. Many of the women were fed raw opium to help them endure the long hours of arduous work. This has been a common practice for thousands of years.

Farmers in higher elevations survived better than most, due to a greater source of runoff water from the winter snowpack.

However, their growing season was extremely limited, and only certain crops would grow due to temperature and elevation, and they seldom rotated crop soil. Even basic life sustaining food was very costly, and it was rarely imported. I cannot recall seeing anyone with an overweight problem. A large part of the United States' benevolent efforts in the country were intended to modernize cultivation and irrigation techniques. But most of that technology found its way into clandestine U.S. interests in the regional opium industry, to this day the largest supplier of illegally grown opium.

Our own Professor Kakar lived in a house made of mud and clay and twig bricks. The first year of construction, he and his wife had nothing but a shanty tent, then each year that followed he would build a wall, and after four years the first room was complete, including a domed brick ceiling. After that, every few years another room was added. Just gathering the raw material was a huge task. Finding the clay and twigs and even the water to make the bricks and a clay mortar to hold them together took more time than the actual brick making and construction.

Growing up, Kakar's parents had no money for candles and electricity was nonexistent, and he read by the light from glowing dung and moonlight. To succeed as the head of the Department of Anthropology at Kabul University took incredible drive and determination. He truly cared about this nation and its people; by far he was the most honorable man I met in Afghanistan.

While traveling through the remote parts of Afghanistan, Lee and I kept a careful eye on each other. We used our hotel in Kabul as our home base, and took daily trips out into the countryside. While in Kabul, Dad and I often parted company and ventured out to go shopping, or to just do our own thing. Abdul was assigned to me as a driver and bodyguard, and he kept a watchful eye on me.

***

Through one of the American diplomats my father interviewed, I met some American students who were in Kabul attending an international school. Their diplomat and consultant parents were usually busy and left their children to occupy themselves. We had a mutual attraction for quality hashish, and with Abdul's assistance, the students and I made contact with a local hashish trader who was known for supplying royalty with the finest quality hash in the region. I actually became quite good friends (two intimate afternoons) with a cute blond whose father was an agricultural consultant (CIA).

I secretly purchased a small quantity of Cannabis Indica seeds. Praised and used only by dignitaries and royalty for centuries, this rare plant was forty times more potent than any hemp plant known to the Western World. These seeds would eventually revolutionize the industry back home. One seed in the States would bring a hundred dollars. Unlike bulky hashish or opium, these seeds could be easily concealed. First, I dipped each seed in a resin to seal in any odor. Abdul's wife, who just happened to be a tenth generation tapestry weaver, sewed the seeds into the lining of my corduroy jacket so they were undetectable. I sealed some more with black epoxy into the handle of my movie camera.

As a decoy, in case my father became suspicious of my activities (being a good and caring father), I had Abdul's wife sew some wildflower seeds (that resembled pot seeds) into the lining of my daypack. So if Lee decided to snoop around my things, it was better he find the decoy and call off the search, then to continue searching and find the real thing. If my father knew I was smuggling, he would probably disown me for several days, if not for an entire month. He did not take me on a trip around the world with him so that I could end up dead or rotting in some third world prison.

Lee, during his private time away from me in Kabul, was up to something mysterious. He made several phone calls from the hotel room and went on more than one secret rendezvous in the capital city. Little did my father know that he was playing into an elaborate practical joke, one that his good friend back in the States and I carefully planned in detail, a couple of months before our trip began.

***

On top of a hill overlooking the city of Kabul, Afghanistan's first two hundred-room luxury hotel had opened just two years before. This was the height of the tourist season and yet there were maybe only six other rooms occupied in the entire place. All but two floors were sealed off completely. Impoverished Afghanistan was no vacation destination.

While we were at the hotel, my father and I befriended Navid, an airline representative stationed at the hotel. He was educated in international business and linguistics. Somehow, he was assigned the worst position the airline had to offer, that of being based in Afghanistan. Sitting by a telephone that seldom rang was a waste of his talent. Navid honorably manned his private office at the hotel even though hardly anyone ever visited him there.

Middle-aged, casually dressed and polite, Navid accompanied us on a couple of our day trips near Kabul. There was something going on under the surface, possibly a hidden agenda, one he kept secret from typical travelers like my father and me. What Navid did not understand was that my father was not a typical traveler. We finally asked him to confide in us.

Navid was initially hesitant, but he allowed us to join him on a visit to the prison in Kabul where he had some business to do. Dad, Professor Kakar and I went with him. Abdul drove us.

As we walked into the dilapidated ancient government facility, we were amazed at how rundown and poorly maintained such a place could be. Unfit for human habitation, it was made of thick clay brick walls, with no glass windows, and only metal bars to stop the cold night air from entering the prison cells. There was no way to get rid of the human excrement. It was an open sewer.

Most of the prisoners were Afghans. A small percentage of the inmates who had been caught in various criminal activities, were from Asia, Europe and the Americas. The foreigners were treated with cruelty and disrespect. All of the inmates were extremely undernourished and it was rare if any survived a lengthy sentence.

We were there because Navid needed to speak with two recently incarcerated women. European in origin, both of them were a little over twenty years old. They had been captured with five kilos of hashish in their luggage as they were going through customs at the Kabul airport. The two foreign citizens were immediately brought up before a magistrate and both were subsequently sentenced to ten years in prison.

According to Navid, these two naive female foreigners had been severely beaten, repeatedly raped and abused from the day of their arrest.

Since their incarceration forty-five days ago, Navid had been doing what he could to gain their release. Unfortunately, this airline representative was working outside the scope of his expertise. He was getting nowhere in his negotiations with government officials. Nevertheless, he kept trying in hopes that eventually someone in the government would give in and set the women free.

Since Navid had run out of ideas, he hoped that my father might offer a suggestion or a different perspective on what to do. I thought my father might be trying to teach me a lesson here, but that didn't keep me from my firm resolve to complete my seed smuggling venture. My first impression was that Navid was sincere about the women. No actor I have known could ever fabricate such a sad story and maintain character with a straight face.

During our brief visit to the prison, guards ushered the five of us into a room with chairs and a table. We sat down and waited for the two women. A few minutes later they were escorted into the room and ordered to sit opposite us. The guards stood at the entrance to the room and waited.

Just one glance gave me an idea of the hardship the two women were enduring. They were unwashed and covered with dirt. Their filthy hair was clumped and in disarray. They were bruised and battered, with skin red and purple from the beatings and assaults. Their clothes were nothing more than torn and excrement-stained rags. Even though they stank, we couldn't move away. They could barely walk, and only shuffled. Forty-five days in prison and they were almost dead. Even though Navid smuggled them handfuls of food every day, they showed signs of malnutrition and dehydration. The saddest part of all, was the fact neither one of them lifted their faces. It was as though they wished never to be noticed. They were so utterly disgraced and all hope was lost.

Navid spoke to them, but they could barely answer, because of the damage done to their mouths. Missing teeth, swelling and open wounds made it difficult for them to do more than whisper. In their shame they covered their faces with crippled fingers that had been broken and not properly set. And then they began to cry. It was difficult to look directly at them and even more difficult to look away. These two once lovely women had aged ten years in just a matter of weeks.

Navid could only reassure them that he was making progress, and had an audience with a government official in a couple of days. But he was lying; we knew there was no such appointment. He did not have the heart to tell the women that there was no progress.

Navid had met them while they were in the dining room of the hotel a week before they were captured. He believed that whatever they were accused of, what they now suffered was inhumane and unacceptable. He visited them every day and took food from his pockets and placed it in their hands. They ate the food as fast as he could hand it to them. After a few days he only brought soft food that did not require chewing. They thanked him and would pray that he'd make another visit the next day. And he promised, and continued to promise, that he would never give up.

As the two women were escorted from the room, they briefly looked directly at Dad, Kakar, Abdul, and me. One of the women had absolutely no expression on her face and the other gave us a look of sadness and utter despair. It broke my heart.

As soon as the women left the room, Navid covered his face, slowly lowered his head to the table and cried for several minutes. I could only assume he had done this every day for the past forty-five. We tried to console him, but there was nothing we could say that made the situation any better. I looked over at Dad and he looked at me and we both stared at Kakar, then all three of us looked at Abdul. All of us had tears streaming down our faces.

On the drive back to the hotel, nobody in the vehicle said a single word. I knew the expression on my father's face for I had seen it many times. Something was brewing.

***

After checking for messages at the front desk, Dad entered Navid's office. The Professor and I followed, but stood in the opened doorway and waited. Navid was sitting at his desk, staring into space.

Dad walked over and sat on the edge of his desk. "You know, sometimes I will be working on a plotline for a new book and the harder I try to make something happen, the further I get from a solution."

Navid came out of his trance and looked at my father.

"And I get this monumental feeling that my writing project is doomed to failure. But rather than surrendering to failure, I become angry at myself, and I tell myself not to give up. Yet, I realize that sometimes it is important to regain my focus. Otherwise, I will fall deeper and deeper into a black hole. So, I get up out of that chair and go for a walk or play with my kids or make love to my wife. And then, maybe a day later, I come back and sit in the chair. And out of nowhere I reach up and grab an idea out of thin air, and I load a blank piece of paper into the typewriter. Before long all the worries in my world are gone. Problem solved." Dad reached over and placed his hand on Navid's shoulder. "You've been too close to this problem for the past month and a half. Go home. Take a couple of days off. I will have Abdul bring food to the two women at the prison. And when you have found the inspiration and resolve you need, then march right back into this office. Contact those people you would rather not talk to and persuade them to see things your way."

As soon as Navid left the hotel, Dad marched directly into the hotel manager's office. Hovering over the manager's desk, Lee asked, "How many separate phone lines run through my suite?"

"Mr. Uris, there are four phone jacks in your suite," replied the manager.

"Have three more phones delivered."

"I will have them installed before the hour is out," the manager said.

"We will need round the clock room service. Another couch and a bigger desk, and another coffee table, an English typewriter and paper, pens and pencils and markers and up to date local, country and world maps, and possibly a globe. See if you can round up any foreign language-to-English dictionaries. Finally, any possible phone numbers or contacts you might have in the government or with big business interests in the country. Two women's lives are at stake and time is running out." Dad shook the manager's hand. "I would appreciate any help you can offer. And thank you."

"Most certainly, Sir." The manager wrote down the requests. He was well-read, and familiar with my father's books. "If I may enquire, does this deal with the two female prisoners, the ones Navid has been trying to get released?"

"Then you understand the importance." Dad added, "My daughter is twenty-four." My father was showing that he had a vested interest in women that age—besides the one he just married.

"I have three daughters. Anything you wish, it will be done."

Dad turned to Professor Kakar. "First of all I need you with me every step of the way. This is your country and you understand the people and how it is run. I need phone numbers of every high-ranking government official in Afghanistan—religious leaders, military leaders, landowners, warlords, and businessmen. I want to know who owns what, who owes what to whom. And tell your wife you won't be home for dinner." Dad smiled and added, "Please."

The Professor smiled. "Absolutely. I understand precisely."

Lee turned to me. "Son, order up some coffee and sandwiches to the room. We have some phone calls to make."

***

Lee and I went up to the room and minutes later three more phones were installed. The hotel staff delivered the couch, a couple more chairs, maps, a typewriter and everything we asked for.

My father commandeered the couch and one coffee table and I sat across from him. The Professor sat at a table near the window. Each of us was armed with legal pads and plenty of pens and pencils.

Professor Kakar dove into his task of getting names and phone numbers and investigating other pertinent information.

Lee placed his first call to a friend in Los Angeles, his attorney and business manager Herb Schlosberg. After explaining the situation, Dad added, "Time to call in all debts. I need to know who owes me a favor. I want a list and the phone numbers of all my trusted allies and equally as important a list of those people who are my sworn enemies. I'm looking for any angle and any kind of leverage to wedge between these people. I need to know anyone who will side with me on this issue, and even those who will not. All our contacts with the State Department and the Israeli government, all our foreign edition publishers and any charitable organizations I have helped. I also need a list of any underworld figures that have reached out to me for any reason since my career started. Someone out there has the magic button, and we will get to him or her. I need you to work with me on this from your end. Call me right back with some numbers." Lee was quiet for a moment. Herb must have been talking. "Thanks Pal. And give my love to your lovely wife and the girls. Talk to you soon. Thank God these girls in prison aren't our girls." Lee was a clever sociopath. He knew that by mentioning Herb's daughters (roughly the same age as the incarcerated ones), he was targeting Herb's conscience with a direct hit.

Dad thumbed through his personal phone book and wrote down names and numbers. The Professor, speaking in Pashto, continued to make contacts and wrote down any pertinent information.

"What do you want me to do?" I asked.

Lee handed me a list of twenty names and numbers. "Call these and when you get someone on the line, hand the phone to me. Get ready to take a lot of notes. Be extremely polite, but at the same time persistent, and do not let anyone hang up on you. Do not accept excuses or delays. We are fighting giants. They will try to intimidate and control the conversation. Stand firm and decisive and direct. If they hear fear or intimidation in your voice they will hang up, or hand you off to someone more polite that has far less executive power. If you lose your nerve, remember the girls. That should slap you back in line."

The phone calls started out slow and awkward. And when Dad got just one person on our side, that one person made a call from their end of the world to another person, and then that person jumped on board. And soon the juggernaut that my father inspired slowly left port and headed out into the open seas. My father did not hold anything back. He went into full detail about the abuse the women suffered. My father's intensity cut right through the phone lines and right into the heart of the person being solicited, awakening their conscience, and inspiring them to take the next step.

Lee's master plan was for each person to make at least one call to someone influential that might be able to help.

***

By the time we started our second day of phone calls, there were people calling people in every corner of the world.

I juggled the phone calls as they poured in. "Hello... this is Michael Uris, Leon's son. He is on the other line... it is a pleasure to speak with you, Willy. How are things going with Oktoberfest? (Pause) Oh... that is good news. Hold the line for a few moments... and thank you... your support means the world to Dad." I then turn to Dad and announce, "Willy's holding, said to take your time. He's calling in a debt from an old friend in Pakistan."

A few minutes later another phone rang and I answered, "Hello... this is Leon's son Michael." (Pause) "Senator... nice to hear from you. Your voice is clear, must be on my end." (Pause) "Dad's on the other line." I called over to Dad, "It's Senator... he has a possible solution." I then turned back to the caller. "Dad will be right with you." (Pause) "Oh, you know Dad. If the world becomes a perfect place, he'll move to another planet. (Pause) "Yes, I am very proud of him."

And as one day would end in one part of the world, a new day would begin in another. We worked around the clock without any real rest. Occasionally one of us would doze off only to be awoken minutes later by another incoming call. We followed time zones around the planet. Eventually people were cross-referencing each other and we knew we were on the right track.

Before long, prominent diplomats were making phone calls and ambassadors and representatives were having emergency meetings with people they normally avoided.

Jews talked with Arabs who had tea with Christians who talked with the British who had talks with a personal friend of the Shah of Iran who knew the wife of a diplomat who knew the President of Afghanistan. The French government—well, they hung up on us—but a French businessman knew a Swedish diplomat who had a luncheon with the Turkish ambassador who called a member of the Soviet Politburo who ended up making a phone call to a high-ranking Afghan government official.

Only someone with the influence, cunning and compassion of my father could have orchestrated this grand opera of humanity. And he had done it all while at the same time guarding the women's privacy and anonymity. This experience taught me an invaluable lesson, of how the world really ran, through back room deals with the names of the guilty and innocent rarely spoken out loud so as not to cause retribution or incrimination. Everyone had their breaking point, and with just the right amount of reasoning my father reached their hearts and injected them with just enough compassion to push the right button.

***

Thirty-six hours after we began, Dad rested on the couch, with one eye open and his hand on the phone. Snapping out of another catnap, I sat up and yawned.

"Get ready for another long day," he said with a smile.

There was a knock on the door, and I sprang from the couch to open it. It was Navid. Unshaved and out of breath, he entered the room.

Navid looked around and saw the four telephones and Professor Kakar sitting at the table with his arms crossed and his head cocked over to the side, fast asleep and snoring.

Navid asked, "Why are there four phones?"

Lee stood up and stretched. "Oh, we were having some trouble with the lines. I think it is all cleared up now. Damn hotel phone systems never work. Had one of those all-important phone calls on a movie deal, didn't want to miss it." Dad excused himself and went to the bathroom.

For the next minute Navid looked around the room and realized exactly what had happened. He placed his hand on my shoulder and simply said, "Thank you. I know there was never a movie deal."

I nodded.

"You look like you could use some sleep," he said.

I pointed at the snoring Professor. "Our friend helped quite a bit."

I asked, "Any word..."

"That's why I'm here." He started to tear-up.

Dad left the bathroom and walked over to Navid, "I didn't catch any of that... you sure could use a shave."

"The two women..." Navid took a deep breath.

"Are they alright?" Lee asked.

After a few moments Navid regained some composure. "Not long ago I received a phone call from my contact in the government. Several high-ranking officials were in a frenzy all day yesterday, and well into the night. Two hours ago, someone ordered their immediate release."

Dad's face lit up. "That's great news."

Navid now had tears streaming down his face. "Sentences commuted and all criminal records expunged. The two were immediately transported by ambulance to the airport. Several cars filled with government officials accompanied them. Then, along with a doctor and nurse, they were immediately placed on a waiting chartered jet. Ten minutes later they were in the air and heading home. I was told they never stopped crying from the moment they first heard the news... all the way until the time their flight finally took off from the Kabul airport... and everyone around them, without exception, shared in their joy and elation."

Navid reached out and my father's hand. "Thank you."

My father smiled. "Without you they would still be in prison."

Navid said, "You moved mountains, yet refused to take any credit. I admire that. Somehow you connected with someone influential, who must really love those two women."

My father replied with glassy eyes, "I'm looking right at him."

12

Superman

After a well-deserved rest, the next morning Lee and I packed our bags and headed to the lobby of the hotel. Dad received an urgent message from a Soviet General and agreed to meet with him before we left the country. After loading up Abdul's jeep with our luggage, we checked out of the hotel and headed for the back streets of Kabul.

We soon found ourselves walking into a seedy nightclub that did more business during daylight hours. The dimly lit dungeon resembled a thousand-year-old nomadic tent that had just been invaded by the disco era. Colorful hand woven silk draperies and wool rugs contrasted against the background of plastic beads and smoky mirrors. A jukebox played 'B' side Elvis flops.

Owned by some shady private investors from the Soviet Union, this was a notorious stomping ground and a safe haven for thieves, smugglers, mercenaries, assassins and other such dangerous characters. Most of them were independent contractors without any affiliation or allegiance. Conmen mixed with back street thugs.

Dad and I went into the back room where a man in his mid-sixties awaited our arrival. He was a stout bear of a man with bushy grey hair, thick eyebrows and a chunky mustache, wearing shorts and a safari shirt and hat.

The man greeted my father with a hug and a handshake, "Leon, it is good to see you my old friend!"

"Andrei. You have put on some weight since the last time we met."

"My wife, she is a fine cook." Andrei looked at me and extended his hand. "So this is your son. Your father and I have known each other since 1961, when he visited Moscow. I worked as... as his guide."

"And Andrei and I have corresponded ever since," Lee said.

"Corresponding about what?" I asked.

"Shut up, Son." My father said, "Andrei and I have urgent business."

"Yes, my old friend, we must hurry. The flight for Moscow is being held at the airport for me."

Andrei suddenly became very nervous and quickly emptied the contents of a weathered briefcase onto the table. For the next twenty minutes he carefully explained each of the official military documents, maps, charts, and timetables. Everything was written in Russian and most of the documents were stamped with what looked like official seals.

Andrei was a Soviet defector who, wanting to pad his retirement, willingly showed us the pre-invasion strategy for the eventual Soviet invasion of Afghanistan, and how the Soviets were going to use the country as a stepping-stone for marching through Pakistan and all the way to the Arabian Sea, effectively cutting Asia in half.

Over the past few years the Soviets, in what were purported to be humanitarian efforts, already started building modern medical facilities, power plants, military outposts, dams and waterworks, highways, bridges and tunnels. This infrastructure was being built in Afghanistan, so that once the Soviets rolled into the country, everything they needed would already be in place.

I pretended to inspect each document even though they were in Russian and I couldn't understand a word. Everything that Andrei said made perfect sense, as the entire time we were in Afghanistan I kept wondering why the Soviet Union took such an interest in this backward and desolate place. Now Lee had involved me in an international spy adventure.

While Andrei fumbled through the paperwork, Dad told me the story of how he first met Andrei in Moscow in 1961 while researching *Armageddon*.

"As agreed, a million German Marks will be wired to your Swiss bank account, but only after I arrive safely in the United States and hand over the documents to my government," Lee said.

"We must toast, Leon, to your safe arrival back in the States." The General ordered a couple of shots.

The bartender handed a shot glass to each of them.

Without hesitation Andrei toasted, "To life!" Then he quickly gulped down the shot.

My father, having sniffed at his glass, hesitated and then put it down on the table.

Almost immediately, Andrei grabbed his throat and began to choke. He gasped for air and his head slammed onto the table. While Dad frantically checked for a pulse, he ordered me to abandon Andrei's briefcase and place the stack of documents under my jacket, and then swiftly take them out to the jeep. I did exactly what my father told me, and waited in the jeep with Abdul.

***

A minute later, Lee calmly exited the disco and climbed into the jeep. Dad casually informed me, "I thought something was off. I should have warned Andrei, but it didn't register until it was too late."

"I thought he just had a heart attack or some kind of seizure."

"He was murdered! Both shot glasses reeked of ammonia. We had better hurry and get to Pakistan."

I still had my daypack with me that I carried all the time. I suggested, "I'll empty my daypack and place the documents inside. That way I can keep them with me at all times, at least until we arrive back in the States."

Dad said, "I was thinking the same thing. Keep some food in it and if anyone becomes suspicious, just take out some food and eat it."

"Sure, Dad. You can count on me."

The first challenge was to get to the Pakistani border and somehow clear customs without being detained, arrested, interrogated, tortured or shot or hung. Luckily for us, Abdul knew the back roads leading out of Kabul and before long we arrived at the Khyber Pass. In order to hasten our escape at the customs depot Abdul paid off the head official, who just happened to be a second cousin, with a very generous bribe, and we quickly headed onto the world's most infamous mountain pass.

With a mystique of its own, the Khyber Pass was a very long and twisty narrow roadway that wound through the mountains separating Afghanistan and Pakistan. Of great historical significance, both ancient and modern armies dreaded traveling this hazardous highway. Alexander the Great and his army of thousands barely survived the perilous journey. The local population who had control over the mountain pass, and who had done so for the past few thousand years, still rode on horses and lived in villages that resembled those of centuries ago. With an atmosphere reminiscent of the Wild West, this rural area was not the place to be found after dark. At night this pass transformed into one of the most lucrative lawless and sinister regions in the world, harboring smugglers and many others engaged in illegal activities. If there were any place where time truly stood still, it was the Khyber Pass.

Abdul raced the Land Rover over the narrow two-lane mountain roadway. In Afghanistan the vehicles drove on the right side of the roadway. In formerly British-ruled Pakistan the vehicles drove on the left side. There were no rules along the Khyber Pass, and, like a giant game of chicken, vehicles dodged each other just avoiding a collision at the last second. Driving the pass is terrifying under any circumstance. Stranded vehicles riddled the roadside ditches after being forced off the narrow highway by opposing traffic. Lee was shaking and sweating. He looked like he was going to have a heart attack.

I distracted myself by filming movies out the window. After a long hour of white-knuckle terror, we arrived at our destination.

In Peshawar, we bid farewell to Abdul and both of us gave him a sizable gratuity. I will never forget his loyalty and sense of compassion. He was the one who offered, that if we could not succeed in freeing the two women from the prison, that he would head an assault team to rescue them. Naturally, my father placed his offer on hold, stating he did not wish the women to become international fugitives. On the other hand, my father swore that if his own efforts failed, he would stand by Abdul's side during the assault.

***

Dad and I checked into our four-star hotel, a remnant of the British Empire that should have been abandoned decades ago. After ten days in Afghanistan, this hotel, rundown as it was, was a relief. Finally, there was something vegetarian besides bread and potatoes for me to eat. The bread came with edible butter and I poured yellow pea and mushroom gravy over the potatoes.

***

As I lay in bed, I was worried about the seeds in my jacket lining and camera handle. It would be no laughing matter if I ended up in a third-world prison and faced the same fate as the two women in Kabul, or got thrown into a US prison to have Bubba, Clem and Luther as my cellmates. Even one night would be an eternity.

However, I did laugh to myself about Andrei's 'murder.' I was not concerned in the least about his fate. I knew the entire grand performance with the Soviet invasion plans was a hoax perpetrated by my father. Andrei wasn't dead. I'd seen the fog of his breath against the glass table after he had supposedly stopped breathing.

My father thought he put one over on me, and that he had me fooled into carrying top-secret spy documents across the globe to Los Angeles. This was not the case. I planned to have him go on thinking that I believed I was smuggling Soviet military plans through Pakistan, Australia, and New Zealand. Dad had another trick up his sleeve, using the Soviet plans in my backpack as a decoy, when all along he was carrying real Soviet invasion plans in microdot form hidden in his electric shaver's case. Truth be told, it was a double cross, and both the documents I was carrying in my backpack, and the microdots he thought were real, were both part of an elaborate practical joke Dad's best friend, Bob Alterman, and I planned out in detail. The microdots Lee was so worried about came from a business associate of Bob's who sold irrigation valves to Third World countries and just happened to be in Afghanistan when we were there.

So, instead of me worrying all the way back to the States, Dad would be the one to suffer the very same fate he wanted to place on my shoulders. The fact Dad's best friend planned the entire hoax gave me a warm fuzzy feeling, one that no matter how pissed off my father would become once he found out what really happened, I could throw my hands up in the air and declare, "Bob's expecting your call." Just saying that, Dad would know he'd been had.

I never let go of the daypack containing the phony secret documents. I saw that my father was proud of me and that's what really mattered. I didn't come on this trip to outwit my father. I came because I desperately needed him in my life. I only thought, that if I played his silly games, that he would for once in my life look up to me. That is all I ever wanted, to be his friend, to know he loves me unconditionally, no matter how I acted in the past.

The next morning, we toured Peshawar and the surrounding areas. Hundreds of thousands of impoverished people lived on top of each other in makeshift shanty villages, wooden shacks, mud huts, and dilapidated buildings.

On our trip, we wore simple, casual clothing and never pulled out an eyeful of cash. Lee never flaunted his money or fame. He was easy to travel with. What I liked most about this journey with my father was the enjoyment he got from even the simplest of things: a good meal or a funny joke. He was well aware that there was a dark side to humanity, but he basked in the positive. He felt his purpose was to lift people out of the desolation of circumstance, and share with others the secrets of gaining their own independence and freedom. This was the side of him I most admired.

***

After a couple of days of wandering the sidewalks and sewers of Peshawar, my father and I caught a flight to Lahore, on the eastern border of Pakistan, near India. On the flight, we met a couple of television crews who were going to Lahore to cover a border dispute with India.

West Pakistan and India were headed toward war with each other over the disputed territory of East Pakistan. It wanted independence and to be renamed Bangladesh. We stayed at the Inter-Continental hotel that was very close to the border. Though I enjoyed doing research with Lee, the danger of a war zone upped the ante. Even though I had already heightened my reality with the drug smuggling, my imagination expanded tenfold when I thought I might be trapped on the front lines of an international conflict. To add to the excitement at the hotel, in came the national football team returning from an all-important international match. They were treated like royalty and followed by a large group of fans. Everywhere we turned there was adventure, danger, romance and intrigue.

At Lee's suggestion, I stored my daypack with the (phony) Soviet invasion plans in a safety deposit box in the hotel safe. I was making a big deal of keeping the daypack with me and I think Lee was finally growing weary of my ultra-paranoid sneaky James Bond spy antics. I was like a puppy constantly letting my master know I had it. By telling me to put the pack in the safe, he was letting me know that he knew I had the bone, but it was time to give the whole thing a rest.

***

Wherever Dad and I traveled, we were assigned an expert who was knowledgeable about the surrounding area. In Lahore, in addition to the basic tour, we met with various people: historians, museum curators, and cultural attachés. Our guide was a sociologist who traveled and researched extensively throughout Asia and the Pacific. George resembled a bullish George Reeves, the ill-fated actor who played Superman on television in the fifties.

Our Professor George had a chip on his shoulder. I figured his doctoral dissertation must have been on the advantages of being an incredibly maladjusted asshole. Everywhere we went he was not only insulting, but also aggressive and short tempered. On a positive note, the highly educated professor had a brilliant, informative and interesting mind.

I kept a watchful eye on our belligerent guide in hopes of finding a way to communicate with the man trapped under layers of antagonism. Analyzing him became a hobby. It kept my mind off real dangers. I still hadn't talked to Lee about Margery and I was putting it off. That would likely be more explosive than the discomfort of dealing with a Rhodes scholar who acted like a pushy child.

After spending a few weeks with an adolescent like me (I say this because Dad considered me an adolescent until I turned forty-five), Lee relished the opportunity to bond with someone with a college degree. Lee was always seeking out intellectuals and considered himself one of them even though he had dropped out of high school to join the Marines. Dad, having been away from his wife for a few weeks, found no reason not to join George's 'He-Man Women Hater's Club.' Together my misguided father and his new super buddy enjoyed the pleasures of macho male supremacy. They bullied their way through their days in Lahore.

They even went so far as to arm wrestle each other at breakfast, lunch and dinner.

My father was not a bitter and angry man like George. I suspected that despite the bonding, Lee had a secret agenda. It was as though my father was cheering George on, in a noble quest to beat the crap out of my abstract ideologies. George had become my father's advocate and knight in shining armor. He vowed to defeat any original thought left within me, and transform my reasoning into a clone of George's mental superiority, and in doing so, my father would win the final battle between us, by using an advocate to do his dirty work.

They ganged up on me at every chance possible, smashing and slapping my mind around as though it were a tennis ball in a match from hell—General Patton and a pissed-off Superman going up against Gandhi. They debated with me as though I was a confused follower of some irrational cult, and declared everything I said to be nonsense.

If I were antagonistic and insulting, they would say that I didn't believe in my own ideologies. These men dealt in empirical theory and I dealt in ethereal concepts. These two drunks took turns using me for verbal target practice. They ate blood rare steaks that flapped like tongues from their laughing mouths and claimed that I was physically inferior and mentally deficient, because I dined on broccoli, rice and tea.

George was having a bad influence on my father. My brother would have easily held his own with these two intellectual hardball players. Dad thought that my theoretical concepts of esoteric reasoning lacked clarity, purpose, and function. I never put up much of a fight and found strength in tolerance. I let them talk uninterrupted even though my conscience begged me to object. The more passive I was, the angrier they got.

One thing that always worked in my favor was my ability to

stay cheerful. I had bad days and, like most people, felt depression at times but in general, when I was with my father, it was easier to be happy than be scolded for not being happy. What really bothered him was how to fight a battle with a son who did not play by his rules.

***

Some soldiers guarding a border outpost leading into India thought we were spies, mainly because the Professor, Dad and I all had Indian visas stamped into our passports. Also Dad photographed and I filmed several activities at the border crossing. The guards threatened us at gunpoint and confiscated all the film in our cameras. George became upset and yelled at the guards who subsequently hit him on the back of the head with a rifle butt. George was knocked to the ground, only to leap to his feet and tackle a different guard. The other dozen guards swiftly came to the rescue, taking turns in gently poking at poor George with their rifle barrels as he lay on the ground. They weren't aggressive enough to cause real physical damage and showed no real intent to harm the belligerent foreigner. George ended up bribing the guards. And then we walked away.

***

That afternoon I was in the crowded outdoor tea garden of the hotel reading a book and having a proper cup of tea, and enjoying the sunlight. Hasnaa, a beautiful Pakistani woman whom I had met on the flight to Lahore, asked if she could share the table with me. She was a translator assigned to some television newsmen by the Pakistani government. We had talked on several occasions around the hotel lobby.

Hasnaa, which meant beautiful, was beyond any normal definition of attractive. She was slender and perfectly proportioned, taller than many of the Pakistani women I had seen. Her dark complexion combined with European features enhanced her beauty. Speaking proper British English, her voice was soft, sweet, and innocently seductive.

***

I was attracted to her and I wanted her to know it so I asked her if there was anyone special in her life.

She winked. "He is sitting across the table from me."

This was going to be fun. There we were in a foreign place and not likely to meet again. It was a moment ripe with possibility. Hasnaa was ten years older than I was. And I was captivated by everything about her. She was like an oasis in the middle of the desert.

"Surely you have been in every male's sight in this part of the globe."

She took a sip of her tea. "I recently called off an engagement."

"What went wrong?"

She took a deep breath and looked at some nearby flowers. "A prominent government official, a few years older than me. He'd been married before. A friend of mine discovered him hiding out with a prostitute while pretending to be at an emergency meeting out of town." She looked at me. "Was that harsh of me calling off the engagement without even listening to his side of the story?"

"He'll come crawling back to you on his hands and knees. To lose someone as beautiful as you would drive any man insane. A little temporary insanity should do him good."

She smiled. "Being with you has cheered me up. Tell me, how are things going with you and George?"

I sipped some tea and faced the afternoon sun. "George is a pain in the ass. I've spent most of my time in Lahore trying to understand him. You worked with him before, as a translator. What's wrong with him?"

"You and your father will figure it out, I have faith in you."

"You say that as though there is something you want to tell me about George. I suppose if it was important you'd tell me."

"George is wounded and running scared. We all care about him. But nobody has been able to unlock his secret."

"Then I suspect George being assigned to my father and me was no accident."

She winked at me.

"My father thinks you were coming onto him on the plane."

She laughed, blushed, and shook her head.

We talked and laughed and flirted for another hour. Even though we lived worlds apart, we had a lot in common. We continued to talk. I hadn't felt this comfortable since I'd left Los Angeles for Vienna (make that... since I was in Istanbul with our guide's mistress's sister, no, make that... since I spent those afternoons with the cute student I met in Afghanistan). At times Hasnaa and I didn't say anything at all, and just gazed at one another.

Her eyes were a brilliant phosphorescent blue and looking into them was like diving off the edge of a waterfall, and landing in a warm pool.

My father and I were not scheduled to leave Lahore for another couple of days. This opened up an opportunity for Hasnaa and I to casually become better acquainted, so we agreed to meet in the hotel bar for a drink after dinner. Other than shopping and a little sightseeing, nothing important was scheduled for the remainder of our stay. Dad's friendship with George kept both of them occupied and my father would hardly notice if I slipped away.

***

That night Dad, George, and I joined up with the television newsmen in the hotel restaurant to celebrate another day of not being shot. And after my father and George ate steaks so thick it took four waiters to carry them to our table, we all ventured over to the hotel bar where an informal party for the Pakistani football team was in full swing.

In the lavish bar area, the Professor kept the newsmen occupied with boisterous accusations of how the Pakistani's were responsible for instigating a possible all-out war with India.

While waiting for Hasnaa to arrive, I joined my father and we moved to a table away from the commotion.

I sipped on my Roy Rogers' soda through a straw. "George is hiding something."

"That's obvious. Why do you think I teamed up with him like I did. Had to gain his confidence somehow."

"So that's your excuse for being an asshole."

"I'm your father, I don't need an excuse for being an asshole." Dad smiled. "Something happened to George. Derailed him, and now he thinks its all the justification he needs to be reckless."

"He's too smart to act like such a shithead."

"George reminds me of a Marine sergeant I knew in the war, meaner than the devil himself. He pushed everyone around, never apologized or backed down. During one of the landings, he rushed out under enemy fire and nobody could stop him, or even wanted to. Just ran headfirst right into certain death. Didn't know any other way to end it all. No one thought him a hero. I haven't been able to get through to George, would you like to give it a shot?"

Dad sipped on his scotch. I winked, and then looked out the window at the nearby brightly lit barricade built to keep people away from the Indian border.

I asked, "Does it bother you that I see the world differently?"

"It would bother me if you didn't."

"Dad, even though we are the best of friends, we always have issues. Yet it is the same things that keep us together that threaten to tear us apart."

"That is life." Dad sipped on his drink.

"We are intelligent, at least I think we are. Why do we need conflict?"

"None of us see the world from exactly the same perspective let alone analyze that data with the same mind. Conflict is inevitable, in some relationships more than others. It depends on the individuals. Even when you think there is no conflict, look closer—everything has an action and a reaction, a counterbalance, a move and a countermove. Opposition is conflict." Dad smiled. "You and me, we always make up. If you think of conflict as normal behavior it will not agitate you as much."

I nodded my head. "You're smarter than you look."

Dad said, "That woman you are seeing tonight is stunning. Careful, those freaky blue eyes could hypnotize you."

"I'm counting on it."

"Well, don't fall in love with her. I know how you are with older women."

I gave my father a stern look. "Hasnaa is about the same age as Margery." I caught myself, "My mistake, her name slipped out."

"No. I slipped up, about your attraction towards mature..."

I interrupted, "Thanks for slipping up, but I don't want to fuck with you when you're drunk. Not on this subject. It's not fair to either one of us." I continued to glare at my father.

"Thank you, Sweetheart." Dad thanked the waitress for delivering fresh drinks. He turned to me. "Fair enough. Let's wait until I'm sober, or someday thereafter."

***

A large number of Pakistani fans that were celebrating with the national football team turned their interest towards Professor George and the newsmen. The newsmen sat at George's table, all eight of them. The athletics team and their dates sat at the next table. The excitable fans sat at the surrounding tables.

Debating and drinking, everyone became excited about the probability of war between India and Pakistan. George and the newsmen condemned Pakistan's aggressive behavior and sided with India who took a significantly more passive stance in the potential conflict.

Before long the drunken pissing match became louder and more out of control. Dad and I took our drinks and headed over to listen to the debate.

George stood up and faced down a few of the football players and fans. They had also risen from their tables. Finger pointing evolved into a couple of wild swings, and then finally one of the football players leaped into the air and kicked George right on the side of his face. It didn't do too much damage as the kicker wore tennis shoes.

Not even losing his balance, George at first just stood there and rubbed his jaw, but then became wild-eyed and threw a forceful punch to the chest that knocked the player to the floor.

About twenty players and fans joined in the brawl, making it two to one odds. Most of the Pakistanis wore tennis shoes and their preferred method of confrontation was with their feet.

Dad turned to me. "Go sit with the ladies."

I could have taken Dad's advice and sat this one out, but nothing brought me more pleasure in life than defying his orders.

I watched as he entered the ring. Two football fans in finely tailored suits and black tennis shoes took turns landing kicks all over his body. Lee threw a few sharp jabs to their arms and upper body, but respectfully avoided hitting either of them in the face.

***

Hasnaa had just entered the bar area and stood in the corner talking to some of the other women. She scanned the room, spotted me and waved. I did not exactly understand what she wanted me to do, so I did what any ordinary fool would do. I rolled up my sleeves and jumped in to save my dear old dad. I only hoped it would not matter to her that all my opponents were Pakistanis.

In the first few minutes of action, three of my knuckles were busted and covered in blood. It was from intercepting relentless tennis shoe attacks with my fists.

No one went totally ballistic and intentionally struck a blow that might place someone in a hospital. If anyone hit someone in the face, with a kick or a punch, it was probably accidental. For whatever it was worth, everyone fought for some kind of honor and the ladies on the sidelines seemed to watch their mates with pride. This was a gentlemanly boxing and kicking match and no one wanted to damage the facility or overly upset their wives or dates.

My father stood his ground, throwing punches at any target directly in front of him. Like a toy robot that could only hit straight ahead, Lee pivoted around to the next target, and hit again and again. It was as though my father was only hitting a reflection of himself. And everyone else seemed to do the same—fighting his own aggression.

The bartender kept lining up and filling shot glasses along the bar, and whenever a fighter got within grabbing distance he reached out and downed a shot. Worn out, George and my father retreated to stools and shots at the bar and waited for the fighting to stop.

Tables were tipped over and chairs pushed all around the room. Splotches of blood splattered the floors, walls, tablecloths, and furniture.

After ten minutes, most all of the fighters had silently slipped away to use the restrooms or to take a spectator's seat at the bar.

My face was covered with sweat and blood and my one eye was swollen half-shut. I did not at first realize the fighting had stopped. Pivoting, I searched for my next target, imagining myself being in a historical prizefight, barely standing on my feet, ready to throw that one powerful punch that would knock out the unbeatable opponent.

Wiping the bloody sweat from my better eye, I saw a short, skinny Pakistani gentleman standing in front of me. He reached out with an opened hand, one of friendship, offering a handshake. I respectfully shook his hand, and then collapsed into a chair and ordered a well-deserved Roy Rogers.

Battered and beaten fighters wiped the sweaty blood from their faces. We unanimously agreed our little war was over, and never should have been started in the first place. We all came to the same conclusion that, like the conflict brewing between India and Pakistan, that anger and aggression stemmed from an impulsive lack of clear thinking. As if everyone wasn't already boozed up enough, they toasted a round to each other's bravery, and laughed off the whole thing.

***

A vision of splendor and grace, Hasnaa came to my side. I just about kissed her on the spot, which I probably should have done. However, even though I was tremendously attracted to her, I played it cool and smiled as she cleaned off my wounds with a napkin dipped in water. She skillfully dressed my cuts and fashioned an ice pack out of a napkin and then placed it on my swollen eye. With a sweet glance she leaned forward and kissed me on the lips before slipping her hotel room key into my shirt pocket as she whispered, "Midnight."

She left for her room to finish up some paperwork. Dad asked George to come to our suite for a nightcap.

13

Purgatory

After taking a shower and changing into clean clothes, and adding a couple of extra bandages, I went out into the living room of our hotel suite. My father and George were talking. Seeing them all banged up and bruised, I could not help but feel sympathy.

Having an hour and a half wait till midnight and my rendezvous with Hasnaa, I grabbed a soda and joined the two old drunks. We sat on a couple of plush chairs and a couch that overlooked the brightly lit city street.

"Lee, who would have guessed Broccoli Boy had any testosterone in his system at all," George said, lifting his cognac as if in a toast.

Dad looked over at George, and then looked back at me and gave me a simple nod. He excused himself to go shower.

George asked, "Tell me Mike, how come you got involved with all this conceptual philosophical bullshit?"

"I can't prove my theories with intellectual reasoning any more than you can disprove them. But I love a discussion, so don't hold back."

George thought for a few moments. "Why doesn't your individual soul reveal itself in the open?"

I gladly replied to George's first assault, "The soul is surrounded by coverings, like a diamond covered with layers of dirt. The diamond no longer has its original luster and brilliance, and appears to be hidden from sight, but it's there, under the dirt all the same. The soul is hidden under veils of perception that are created by our own mind and senses."

"How can anyone confuse a chunk of dirt with a diamond?"

"Take the sun for instance. The sun shines directly onto the surface of the water, and the light is reflected onto a wall. If you have only seen the sun's reflection on the wall, then you believe that reflection is real, but you are only deceived. Only the sun is real. Appearance is a deception of the mind and our sensory input."

"That's Plato's allegory of the cave."

At first George wasn't impressed with me, or my arguments. I stood up and stretched. George spun his head around and cracked his neck. We talked about the distinction between the mind and the soul, and though George didn't agree with me he seemed to stop looking at me like I was some kind of an idiot. I continued to offer my perspective on what is real and what is illusion, stating that the brain and senses, the mind, and the individual soul are all separately functioning entities. That everything in this universe is constantly changing, from subatomic particles to grander galactic expanses. I explained that everything—within and beyond the spheres of time and space—is interconnected into one colossal finely woven tapestry. And what binds all of creation together is a common thread: that ultimate, binding and creative force that people call by different names, like God or Spirit for instance, where as I consider this universal force to be nothing more than love. And what we perceive on this material level of consciousness is merely what our senses gather and our minds translate. The soul is more of an all-powerful divine observer on this level than a participant. In reality our soul is the diamond.

I concluded with a verse from the Rig Veda:

"None knows whence this creation has arisen, whether He made it or it formed itself; He who surveys it from the highest heaven; only He knows; or maybe He does not."

George wiped away some blood that was leaking through a bandage on his arm. "This is all very amusing. You say what is, by offering what is not." He looked at his watch. "What time is your date?"

"Not till midnight." I smiled. It was now or never for me to drop the bomb. "Tell me George, do you believe in love?"

"It doesn't exist in my world!" He was obviously agitated.

"I'll bet you experienced love at some point in your life, even if you're too stubborn to admit it."

"You don't know what you're talking about." George's face was turning red and he moved away from me. "A time long ago my life was different. I was married. How can love be real if she is no longer in my life? You said love is eternal. Tell me, where did it go?" He stared at me.

Dad stood by the doorway. He had never taken a shower and had been listening in on our entire conversation.

George added, "You don't understand shit!"

"Tough guy. Throwing around all your weight." I pointed at him. "Why Pakistan, what are you running away from, why are you hiding? No matter where you go, you are only hiding from the person in the mirror."

George stared at me. "She was the only thing in this world I ever cared about!" George sat back in the chair. "And she's dead." He knocked back his entire drink and threw his glass down, shattering it on the floor. "Just back off! You don't know what the fuck happened to me!"

"I'm looking right at what the fuck happened to you!" I pointed my index finger at George's face. "I've met a lot of people who actually care about you, but nobody can stand you. Why the act George? You are more intelligent than the angry fool you are portraying."

George drew his right arm back getting ready to throw a punch. Dad stepped in, grabbed his fist, pried it open, and placed a fresh drink in it. George took a swig to calm down.

I sat back on the couch. "Dad, what ever happened to that Marine sergeant, the one in the war?"

"The one who marched blindly into combat? He was shot by the enemy." Dad sat down next to me.

"What drove that guy to the edge?"

"The sergeant's family, all four kids and his wife, died in a house fire. The firemen found the sergeant passed out drunk in the driveway. If he hadn't been drunk, he could have saved them."

Hearing about the fire tragedy, George's eyes glazed over and he went into a trance. Just stared right through me for the longest time. Finally, George faced Dad. "I'm about to throw your son out of the room."

I got up and opened the window. We were on the sixth floor. "I think this is the fastest way. Tell me George, what are you afraid of?"

"I'd rather jump out that window then have to recall my own fucking purgatory."

"We won't let you jump, and you're not walking out that door," Lee said.

George looked at us. "You think you want to know about what's at the heart of this, but you don't. Trust me."

I closed the window and sat down.

***

George stood up and walked over to the window, and looked out at the street below. He turned and faced us. His recounting of events went on for quite some time, being far more graphically descriptive, but here is a summary of his story: "New Guinea. A few years back. In a tropical rain forest, on one of the outer islands, my wife and I lived with a tribe that time forgot. I was doing research, studying their culture. My wife was a nurse and we immersed ourselves into the tribe. They were a warring tribe, who, every few years, raided the neighboring villages. It was nothing more than fear-motivated territorial supremacy. In that part of their world it was a way of life.

"My wife and I lived with them for several months and gained their respect. Most of the time, I understood what motivated them. They lived a simple existence. I don't think they really wanted to be so aggressive towards their neighbors, but they followed tradition.

"My wife also helped others tribes in the surrounding area with medical aid. One day she was at one of the nearby villages, just a few miles away, helping with a difficult birth." George's eyes started to tear up. He sat down on the floor against the wall and looked out the window. George began to speak, but hesitated and took a deep breath. Then, he lowered his head and cried. Dad and I waited.

A minute later, George wiped the tears away. "I came back to our village that afternoon, after a daylong expedition downriver. The tribal leader came up to me. Without any emotion whatsoever, he told me that my wife was dead. His warriors had killed her during a raid on the neighboring tribe. Unfortunately, he gave orders that no one in the village was to be spared, and the warriors took him literally. It was all a misunderstanding. The tribal leader did not know my wife was at the neighboring village, if he had known, my wife would have been spared.

"It was customary when visiting any neighboring tribe to get permission. I was in too much of a hurry to go downriver that morning, and I forgot to speak with the chief. It was my fault she was murdered. The tribal leader never apologized for his actions, nor did he offer a single word of condolence. He only pointed in the direction of the village, and then turned and walked away.

"I ran for several miles, through an overgrown swampy jungle. The tribe had used sophisticated weapons of war: machine guns, shotguns, rifles and handguns. The huts were riddled with bullet holes. When they ran out of bullets, they reverted back to axes, spears, cleavers, bows and arrows, and knives. Every single person had been mutilated beyond recognition. That was how the tribe left their mark of revenge."

Dad and I looked at each other and then hung our heads. I took a sip of my drink and my father, in shock, just looked at his scotch.

"I found my wife in one of the grass huts, along with the bodies of the pregnant woman and a couple of children. If not for small chunks of my wife's fair skin and hair, I would not have known her. Her face was gone. And they had chopped away three of her limbs. I could effortlessly pick up what was left of her body with my thumb and index fingers. One arm was barely attached to her torso. It was shredded and covered in blood, and her wedding ring was still on her finger. I fell to the ground and held her. I screamed and wailed for hours, until my voice was gone. I still scream to this day, if only in silence. The horror of that day haunts me constantly."

George couldn't see through the tears as he looked at us. "I should have killed myself the minute I found her."

Both Dad and I went over and sat down on the floor next to him, one of us on each side of him.

"I carried my wife through the jungle. At times I stumbled and fell over, but I never let go of her. I carried her body into the night, waded through rivers and swamps and finally made it to the ocean shore where I found a canoe. In the moonlight, I tied a boulder to one end of a rope, and the other end around what remained of my wife. I swore to give her a proper funeral at sea. I paddled a canoe out into the water as far as I could go, till I couldn't see land anymore. That is the last thing I remembered."

Dad got up, and returned a minute later with a fresh cognac for George. He took a few large gulps. "Five and a half months after my wife's death, I woke up in the hospital, and was finally conscious of my surroundings. A missionary told me that a native tribe found me on one of the outer islands. I was crawling in the swamp, like a lizard. I was practically dead, diseased, dehydrated, and weighed less than seventy pounds. I was naked, and had open wounds and was completely insane. I was crying and mumbling. The missionary told me more about my condition, but some things are better off unsaid." George shook his head. "The doctors kept me in the hospital for another two months. Don't remember what happened after paddling out to sea. I suppose the missionary was right, some things are better left unsaid."

George briefly glanced at the two of us. He was a total mess. For anyone to relive and relate such a traumatic experience displayed a rare form of courage. It took every ounce of his energy to enter his personal hell and release what had been trapped so deep within. He lowered his head.

Everywhere in the hotel room, you could feel the pure emotion emanating from George. There was no escape from the feelings that evening. How George could have trapped that much grief inside his mind for all those years completely astounded me. Even if but once in a lifetime, a confession like that is seldom made. I understood the intense anguish that surrounded his every waking hour, because I was no stranger to losing a loved one by a tragic fate. I remember holding Margery's lifeless body in my arms, and everything seeming like a surrealistic dream. I understood what George felt earlier, when he said it would be easier to jump out the window than recount the tragedy. Even though that evening I was apparently helping George, ironically, I became trapped in the quicksand of my own memory, unable to avoid my own pain from that night on the mountainside with Margery.

Dad stayed with George. I headed off to the bathroom. One of the bandages on my face was soaked in blood. After washing up, I redressed the wound with a fresh bandage. I looked at my image in the mirror, but could only see a reflection of my younger self, who to that day had not dealt with his own traumatic past. But this was not my night to be consoled; I was here for a greater purpose. I smiled at my swollen eye in the mirror and, if only for the time being, bid farewell to my own personal hell.

George looked out the window. "I shouldn't have exposed her to such a primal culture. She was so refined. But the tribe needed her, as much as she needed them. I could have never taken her away, even if I tried. I remember that morning as I rushed off to go down the river. It was the last time I heard her voice. She said, 'I love my husband.' Those words still echo in my mind, I hear them right now, as though she is right here in this room."

Drenched in his own tears, he concluded, "Tell me how fucked up I am. I don't even have a clue. To recall her beautiful face is rare, only her faceless corpse comes to mind. I'm afraid to wake up in the morning, to go to sleep at night, to even have a thought in my head. Whatever I think about, no matter how distant and unaligned, those thoughts eventually lead back to the day I found her."

With those words George completely lost it and sobbed uncontrollably.

Occasionally, George would stop crying, and yawn. I looked over at my father and he pulled a bottle of his prescription sleeping pills from his pocket. That last cognac had been spiked. Lee realized the demons had been released, and now it was for the best that George slept.

George eventually allowed the crying to work its way through his system, and continued to occasionally yawn. It was now almost midnight. He lay on his back in the middle of the room. I lay down next to him, looking up at the ceiling. My father dimmed the lights and joined us. And the three of us looked up at the dimly lit ceiling.

After a few minutes Lee asked, "How are you feeling?"

George mumbled, "I'm not afraid anymore."

"How so?"

George turned his head towards me. In a soft voice he said, "All the dirt is gone and I only see the diamond. I see my wife the way she used to be, in all her beauty."

"You finally set her soul free," I said.

And with those simple words I glanced over and observed him in dim light. A soothing smile came over his face, and just before his eyes closed, his heart opened up and came back to life. And then he softly whispered, "I love my wife."

14

Flight of the Phoenix - Part I

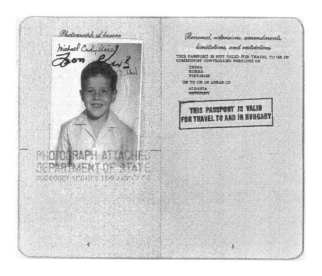

The dictionary definition of PHOENIX: a wondrous mythical bird that arises from its own ashes and flies once again.

The second dictionary definition of PHOENIX: a person or thing that been restored after suffering calamity or apparent annihilation.

The next morning in Lahore...

"I knew you could get through to George, that you and your father could help him," Hasnaa said. Her head was resting on my chest and I was stroking her long, dark hair. "Men are so... suggestible. I talked with George yesterday afternoon, and told him that you thought he was coward and were afraid to have a philosophical debate. George knew all along, that you were going to force his hand. I am certain he was counting on it."

"It all makes sense now. Thanks for setting us up."

"Mike, I notice a sadness about you. Was that connected to the experience with George?"

"No." I softly kissed her. "While in purgatory with George, I had a good look around. I didn't like what I saw, it wasn't easy for me to go there."

Hasnaa whispered, "If you ever find yourself running, remember George, and how it is better to stand and face your fears than run away."

I snapped out of my funk. "What about you and me, did that work out as planned?"

"Far better." She smiled. "Truth is, I wanted to kiss you the moment I met you."

***

Lee spent his remaining time in Lahore with George. My father and his friend went swimming and played tennis and golf, and even danced with some beautiful women at a nightclub. George even went on rounds around town to make amends to a few people that he had wronged over the past couple of years. My father was right there with him to witness his return to the human race.

***

Our next stops were Karachi, Sydney, and all of New Zealand. While in Auckland, we bought a Newsweek Magazine that contained quotes from Lee's Sydney news conference. Much to his dismay, the editors at Newsweek misquoted his words about the subservience of women. Dad was worried that Jill would take the Newsweek statements the wrong way, so we skipped our final rest stop in Tahiti and I made arrangements to leave directly for the United States.

While Dad took a nap to calm his nerves, I secretly called his friend Bob Alterman, and he booked us a flight that was leaving in two hours for Honolulu. It was a chartered medical flight on a full sized jetliner, with only a handful of passengers and a skeleton crew.

The midnight shuttle flight carried only six passengers. Lee and I sat in the bulkhead seats in the front row of First Class. Of the four others on this night flight, a critically ill man was being medically transported on a portable hospital bed; a doctor, nurse, and a traveling companion accompanied him. The four were situated in the rear coach compartment.

The flight from Auckland to Honolulu would take nine hours and arrive at two in the morning. After a brief stop to unload the patient, the nearly empty flight would reach its final destination in Los Angeles.

On the flight to Honolulu, Lee kept busy reading a stack of notes that was a foot tall. I helped him sort out papers and film negatives. Then, I went up to the galley and talked to the crew while the flight attendant made me a sandwich. Lee continued with his work. I returned to my seat and found my father's head cocked over and he was snoring. I walked up and down the aisle to stretch my legs. Somewhat bored, I asked the stewardess about the person in the back of the plane with the medical condition. Her story was interesting and it invoked my curiosity.

A few minutes later I returned to my seat. Eventually, Lee woke from his nap.

Dad always felt it was his privilege and duty as a good father to lecture me. "Son, respect comes in two forms. It is given and earned. For all the actions you've done, weighing the good and the bad, I've only given you my respect. The only way you can earn my respect; is to sacrifice everything you have to stand up for what you know is right."

"Respect is respect, given or earned." I laughed, "Keep splitting atoms and one day your world will become a nuclear wasteland. Face it, you and I think differently about some things."

"More like most things. In time you'll see the world as I do."

"You mean I'll never be normal?"

"Don't fool yourself. You never wanted to be a face in the crowd."

"That's all I ever wanted. But you're right, I am unusual, just the way you molded me. The way I look at it—you are the prototype and I'm the improved model. In fact, I'm going to prove the difference in the way we think."

"This should be interesting." Dad rolled his eyes as he rubbed his forehead.

"Thoughts can be transmitted and received, from one mind to another. It's basic metaphysics and not as complicated as you think."

"I must have really fucked you up as a child."

"I am going to write down five things. By the time we land in Honolulu, those things will have manifested, in some form, before your very eyes."

"They'd better be unusual."

"They will be." I took a paper and a pen out of my pocket and wrote: champ, private school, upside down transparent dome, tribal dancing and singing a lullaby." I folded the paper, handed it to Lee, and he put it in his pocket.

I added, "By the way, those items were just transmitted to me from another person on this flight, into my mind, in the form of a vision."

"God... don't condemn me to hell because my son is insane."

I patted my father on the back. "Get that dollar ready."

The stewardess came by. "We have a lovely steak being prepared."

I mentioned, "Thank you, not for me. Maybe the woman traveling with the patient in the back might wish to come up and take my place."

"That's thoughtful, Son."

The stewardess nodded. "I'll go ask her."

A couple of minutes later, the stewardess returned from the back of the plane and told Dad, "The woman will join you in a few minutes."

He winked at the stewardess. "Thank you, Darling."

Tired from all the travel activities I excused myself and moved back a few rows to take a brief nap.

When I awoke, I got up and walked forward to where my father was sitting. Next to Dad sat a beautiful woman. Somewhere in her sixties, the refined lady was stylishly dressed and had an air of nobility. Since she and my father were talking, I just waved and continued to the restroom.

I then took a walk to the back compartment of the plane where the ill man lay on the portable hospital bed. Three rows of seats were removed to accommodate the bed and medical apparatus. The patient had balding light brown-grey hair and appeared to be asleep. He also had the same long square-chiseled nose as the woman sitting beside my father. The doctor and nurse were seated a few rows back, engaged in conversation they didn't even look in my direction.

Several machines and monitors surrounded the ill passenger. There were a handful of IV solutions on suspended wire racks. One of the machines pumped air through a clear tube into a mask over his mouth.

I said, "I just came back to see how you were doing. My Dad is dining with your sister. I'm about to go forward to confront her about a vision I just had."

The man barely opened his eyes just a sliver, and looked forward. He didn't move his head other than to blink.

"Sore throat?" I smiled at him. "You want to play blinking, fine with me. One blink for yes, two for no."

The man blinked twice.

"Want me to get your sister?"

He blinked three times.

I thought for a moment, and then asked, "Do you want me to get your sister to do something for you?"

The man blinked twice.

"Why don't you rest, Champ. I'll be back in a few minutes with your sister. I promise. She can sing you that lullaby, the one from my vision."

The man smiled and blinked twice, and then closed his eyes.

I patted him on the shoulder, and then headed towards the front of the plane.

***

Lee and the lady were still talking. Dad sat by the window, and she by the aisle. The stewardess cleared their trays and went up to the forward service compartment. My father introduced the lady to me. Her name was Letje, but I pretended not to already know it.

I sat down in the seat across the aisle from her and asked, "The man back there, on the hospital bed. Is he a relative of yours?"

She answered, "Yes, my twin brother, Hargrove."

"Do you by chance happen to own a pair of wire rimmed glasses? On the left side the lens is round on the bottom half, and there is no top half, just the gold rim going straight across... like an upside down transparent dome?"

Baffled, Dad stared at me.

This totally caught Letje off guard. In fact, she practically choked on her wine. After coughing and clearing her voice she abruptly faced me. In a bewildered tone she said, "Not since I was eighteen, over forty years ago. I had astigmatism and a wandering left eye, and the only way I could read or see anything close up in focus was with those glasses. How did you know?"

"Lucky guess." I pointed at her left eye. "I noticed the slightest wandering in your left eye when you looked at me."

"Very observant." She turned to my father. "He's rather sharp. No one has noticed my wandering left eye in years."

The stewardess came by and filled their wine glasses. Letje smiled at my father. Since the glass was filled to the brim, she took a rather large sip of wine.

"I think Champ wants you," I said.

She spit up an entire mouthful all over my father. Good thing it was white wine. In a surprised voice she exclaimed, "What?"

"Champ..."

"I haven't called Hargrove Champ since the academy."

She helped me wipe the wine off of my father.

"A private school? In New Zealand?" I asked.

"Yes..." She sighed and then shook her head. Letje asked me, "What else do you know?"

I answered, "One day you were in a park with other students, watching Maori dancers. Champ was with you."

Dad realized I already spotted four of the five items in the bet we made, and behind her back so she wouldn't see, he raised four fingers and nodded his head at me.

Letje became upset. "What's going on here?" She looked at me. "First the glasses. I fell for that. Now you bring up my brother's nickname and Maori dancers Hargrove and I watched while we were in boarding school over forty years ago? Explain yourself young man!"

Luckily Dad stepped in. "Reads too much Sherlock Holmes if you ask me. My son outguesses me before I even have a question."

Letje just sat in her seat and stared straight ahead. She turned to Dad and said, "That's malarkey." Letje then asked me, "Now, be honest. Did Hargrove talk to you?"

"No, he didn't say a word. But he blinked," I said.

"The doctor said his twitching and blinking are just involuntary muscle spasms. The eyes never actually open." She admitted, "He's been in a coma for well over a year, closer to two." Letje stared at the overhead light. "I was taking him back to Honolulu. His wife passed on recently. The doctors give Hargrove less than four months to live. His brain and vital organs are shutting down. It's only a matter of time." Lowering her head she began to softly weep.

"Champ isn't in a coma," I said. "He looked right at me."

Dad covered his eyes with one hand. "Jesus Christ, Son. This is not a good time."

I turned to Letje. "In my vision, the day of the Maori dancers at the park, your brother was sad and you helped him."

"What vision?" She stared at me. "How did I help Hargrove?"

"I had a vision when I was napping. You were younger, but I recognized you and your brother from your unique noses. The vision is how I learned everything about you and your brother. In the vision you sang a lullaby to your brother. You transmitted those thoughts to me, like radio waves—I simply received them."

"I'm sorry, Letje," Dad rubbed his hand over his forehead and rolled his eyes. That was his way of letting me know that if he could throw me out the window—even though we were thirty-seven

thousand feet up—he would. "Mike has this—small problem with..."
I knew what he wanted to say, but he caught himself. He wanted to
end that sentence with the word 'sanity.' He believed that the thing
he was so afraid of, that I'd lose all touch with reality, had finally come
to pass. "I think this time he stepped over the limit. And I apologize."

She pointed her exquisite finger at me. Her rings glinted in the
dim light. "Do you have any idea how demented you both sound?"

"There's nothing wrong with me. This really happened. I did have
this vision. It's as real as this." I picked up a book that was beside my
father and waved it in the air.

"Letje, trust me," Lee said. "I understand your apprehension, but
maybe we both need to stop, and listen to my son."

"I don't know. This magical thinking isn't really my cup of tea."

I said, "None of this is important. What you believe. What I
believe. What's really important is that you think your brother is in a
coma, and I know he isn't."

Letje pointed her finger at me and raised her voice. "You are lucky
your father is here, otherwise I would slap you right across the face!"

I stood in the aisle, facing her. "Go on. Do it. Get it out of your
system," I said. I then pointed to the back of the plane. "Sing the
lullaby to your brother."

We stared at one another for a few moments.

"I..." Letje was completely confused. She sat down in her seat. "I
don't remember the words."

"I remember them from my vision," I said.

Dad whispered to me, "You really did it this time. I hope you're
proud of yourself."

I wondered if I should stop right there. Lee not only thought I was
crazy, it proved to him I was an insensitive prick.

"Dad, this time, please side with me."

"I'll deal with you later. Disappointing her is what I am concerned
about right now."

Dad stood up and reached out for Letje's hand. Hesitantly, she took it and stood up. Together they walked back to the rear compartment. I followed. Dad sat down in a seat near the hospital bed.

The doctor and nurse were still sitting a few rows back.

Letje and I stood right next to Champ, one of us on each side, by the head of the bed.

And then she followed my lead and we began to softly sing, "You are my Champ and always will be..."

Slowly, Champ opened his eyes. They shifted toward me. She reached out and touched his face. He turned his head and faced her, and then he slowly reached up and moved the mask to the side. Tears began to roll out of his eyes as he smiled at his sister. She started to collapse, but my father rushed to her side and put his arm around her.

Seconds later, Dad approached the preoccupied doctor. "Your patient is no longer in a coma."

With that, the doctor and nurse sprang from their seats. They checked Hargrove's vitals and confirming the patient was in stable condition, they eventually returned to their seats and conversation.

My father shook his head, and hesitantly slipped a folded dollar into my hand. "I wouldn't have believed it if I hadn't seen it with my own eyes."

My father sniffled. He leaned over a whispered to me, "You know, Son, for a while I thought you staged this entire deal."

"What makes you think I didn't?" I asked.

"Because not even I'm that clever." Dad smiled at me. "What just happened, was it an accident, or a miracle?"

"Just my way of earning your respect." I winked with a smile.

Dad thought for a few moments. He nodded his head. "For now, let's say you earned my respect. But that doesn't mean you have to stop trying." He patted me on the shoulder, and headed towards the front compartment and his seat.

***

Then, Hargrove turned to me and spoke in a normal voice. "Not bad acting for a guy in a coma. Smart to add the bit with me involuntarily blinking, at any time your father could have glanced back and seen you talking to me."

Letje laughed. "When I spit-up the wine all over your father, it was priceless."

"It was brilliant." I smiled at them. "Thank you for helping me put one over on my father. It's not easy. He has a suspicious nature, but everyone's performance was so spot-on, he's still in the dark."

"I had so much fun, everyone did. The doctor and nurse played their parts well, and acted so surprised when Hargrove snapped out of his coma. As for me, I was a drama major in college, and this was the first time I've acted in decades," she said.

"We've scammed each other plenty, but this humbled Dad like I'd never seen before. He was so nervous when you got upset, but he finally placed his trust in me."

Letje leaned over and kissed Hargrove on the cheek. "You were the shining star, I only hope your bypass surgery goes as well as your acting." She turned to me and asked, "What about Lee, are you going to keep him in the dark, that Hargrove never was in a coma?"

"I'll tell him the truth, maybe, someday."

Letje smiled. "Why spoil the way he feels about you? Savor your win."

Hargrove added, "I saw the way your father looked at you, a special consideration that few sons ever receive. What your father saw in you was a reflection of his better self, his son doing the right thing. He looked up to you. That is real pride."

15

Flight of the Phoenix - Part II

I eventually returned to the front compartment of the jetliner. As I arrived my father was sipping on some coffee. He smiled, placed his paperwork out of the way, and invited me to sit down and have a little talk. Using the words 'little talk' was Lee's way of preparing me for a verbal hurricane. Taking advantage of the moment, I figured the timing couldn't be better, to discuss what we'd avoided for over two years. And from the look in his eyes, I felt he wanted to get past this subject as much as I did.

Dad said, "I'm impressed by the way you handled Letje. Will I ever know the real story behind your vision—the mental projection you received?"

"Believe whatever. If that doesn't work for you, then use your imagination." I offered a smug grin.

"All of that aside, I'm proud of how you dealt with George, Son. More than any father should, I've been worried about your grasp on reality. But I'm not so worried now."

"I don't think you have to be," I said.

I wanted him to think well of me. Lee was able to walk into a room and work a crowd like no one I'd ever seen. He could have handled George on his own; in fact, he'd spent our time in Pakistan laying the groundwork. I had always felt he saw me as an emotional cripple and, by giving me this task, he was dragging me out of the wheelchair. He was putting me on his own level and trying to raise my self-esteem. I tended to avoid situations if I thought I could fail.

I saw my role in life as playing second fiddle to my brother. If blue was his favorite color, I'd have to choose orange. If he was the college bound intellectual, I'd have to be the drug dealing womanizer. I even believed that Lee needed me to be what I was, that he would never want two sons who thought and acted the same.

The year Margery died was a wash out at school. By my senior year, I had started to pull things together and collected the credits I needed for college, but instead of entering junior college, I was off on my forty days around the world with Lee. In the upcoming spring semester, I planned to go to junior college to get the prerequisite credits needed to enter USC or Brooks Institute film school.

Lee said, "You've made a step in the right direction. Now, go to college and become a doctor or a lawyer or something—respectable. Marry a nice girl with an oral fixation and raise a family. I know you can do it. Do it for me. Do something to make me proud."

"But you never went to college," I answered.

"Okay, be a paperhanger like my Dad."

"Grandpa loves you. He's your biggest fan. You give him a reason to wake up every morning."

"He wakes up every morning to annoy me." Lee gulped the last of his coffee.

"Dad, maybe I'll be a paperhanger just to annoy you."

"I shouldn't have dropped you on the head when you were young—all those times." He raised both hands, looked up and waved them in the air. "God I swear, they were accidents."

***

The stewardess came by and asked Dad if he wanted a coffee refill. As soon as she left, my father said, "It always bothers me around your birthday."

I hesitated for a few moments. "I'm glad it bothers you."

"That was cold."

"So was the night she died."

With blood red eyes, Dad stared at me for a few moments. "It isn't easy for me to talk about it."

"You made me promise to never say her name, if I wanted to have a relationship with you. We both know avoiding a problem is the wrong way to deal with it."

"Go on then, Son, tell me what I need to understand."

"I would have expected you to order me to shut up by now. Maybe

I just want to hear you say her name," I sneered at Dad.

"Margery. Now go fuck yourself. I'm not a priest. This isn't about absolution. Neither one of us will ever forgive the other for what happened that night."

"We need some ground rules before I start calling you Doctor Dering." I may have overstepped the line with this statement, but I wanted to make sure that whatever we said from there on out did not destroy our relationship forever.

Dad blasted, "Margery made her own decisions. She knew where the door was. This is the way I see it. I trapped and caged her. She was too delicate. I broke her will. And, she turned to someone who cared, and that happened to be you."

"I was only fifteen! I could barely grow a mustache."

"You always seemed older than your age."

"You grow up much faster when your old man is the fucking messiah."

"I'm not the messiah."

"I figured that out on my own. It took me a while. But I've always looked up to you, Dad. We both drove Margery to her death by giving her no options. She made the wrong decision. Neither one of us saw her emotional instability. I don't believe she was anything more than confused when she pulled the trigger. Whether it implicates or condemns you or me is not the issue, I just had to get all of this out into the open."

Dad said, "You knew what you were doing was wrong. I don't think it's fair to lay all the blame at my door."

"I just want you to accept what you did to destroy her. And I too will learn to live with my bad decisions."

Dad attacked. "If you ever call me Doctor Dering again I will... never mind."

"Go on, say it."

Dad took a deep breath, taking time to sort out things in his mind. "Our relationship survived this far. Considering what we went through, I think we should both be grateful we still have a chance to get it right. Even if we can never come to terms over Margery, know that I blame myself for raising you in my alter image. I mentored you to make the wrong decisions in life, so that I could be there to rescue you, like a hero to save the day. At times I considered you nothing more than a dependent handicapped child crying for attention. Does that bother you? So, now you know how benevolent your father really is."

"I could never be your intellectual equal, but I could become the womanizer in you. That you could respect. You pushed her at me because you didn't know what to do with her. I used her just like you did. She loved both of us, yet you considered her love a burden."

Dad explained, "I loved her—even though I didn't have the patience to understand her."

"Look, Dad—any real conflict between us faded long ago. I only wanted to clear the air, to have the right to say her name. But don't feed me crap about patience and understanding."

"You never had the nerve to stomach what really happened. I carried you down that hill, not because you were half frozen, it was because I broke you."

"Just like you broke her."

"No one survived that evening unscathed," said Dad.

I became calmly enraged. "Margery was a beautiful woman, quiet and sensitive. It was never about disrespect for you. She actually cared about you, and you took her for granted, like she was some slave. Always trying to please you and say the right things and fulfill your every need. *Make my dinner, fuck me, I'm busy, go take care of my son, spend some time with him, get to know him better.* I was the buffer in your life, I knew my place, but when I fell in love with Margery, everything changed."

Lee shook his head. "When you were eleven, you tried to salvage my marriage with your mother. Thinking you were our problem, that if you were out of the picture that our marriage would survive. You paddled out into the ocean to get away from it all. I don't think what you did was the act of a selfish child. And being the buffer between Margery and me—I know it got out of hand, but at the time I honestly believed you were trying to save our marriage. I raised you like a fictionalized character out of my own books, how could I have expected you to act any different?"

I replied, "So don't be surprised when I do really fucked-up shit. It's not easy to bury the truth, or fiction, when they are both staring you in the face every minute of every day. George's nightmare was another wake-up call, and I was transported back in time to that night with Margery. I can't stop that fucking gun blast from echoing in my head. You know what Dad, I'll never get over her death, but I'm glad she died on my birthday. Now I will never forget her, and if that drives you insane, then that is what you deserve."

Lee closed his eyes. "The truth hurts." He then looked at me. "I just wanted to hear it from you."

We sat in silence and stared at each other for what seemed an eternity.

***

The stewardess came by and poured some coffee for Dad. She asked if I wanted anything, and I shook my head. A few moments after she walked away the plane took a sudden dip and the seatbelt sign came on.

After I regained composure from the sudden loss in altitude, I turned and faced my father. He smiled and I smiled back. Dad had listened to my every word and didn't turn them against me. Whatever type of man I decided to be, my father would always be my mentor. "I'm proud that my father took the time to raise me, even if he fucked up, I like the person I turned out to be. Good or bad does it really matter, being a drug addict and a womanizer has had its finer moments."

Dad took a sip of his coffee. "You were always so vulnerable, willing to do anything to gain my respect. I took advantage of that, like I took advantage of Margery. And for me to be ashamed of my own son for being there for her when she needed someone who cared, it only makes me that much more ashamed of myself."

I glanced out at the clouds. I had that feeling of being out of time and space. We were locked there forever, two men caught in a tangle we could never undo. Would talking about Margery change anything? My psychiatrist had once asked me if I had been in love with 'Margery' or 'My father's wife.' I didn't even have to think about it. It was Margery I loved. My shrink had given me absolution then, even if my father never would. If I took my father out of the equation and loved Margery just for herself, then I wasn't as fucked up as I thought I was. I may think I've come to a standstill with my father on the subject, but if my shrink were here, he'd say that life is a learning experience, and as long as you are alive, what you endure today will give you the strength to survive tomorrow.

I turned to face Dad. "I feel stuck in that day, my shitty birthday. That night follows me everywhere."

"The fact that it happened on your birthday shouldn't bother you as much as the fact that it happened at all."

"I know that. But why don't you call me—on that day? You always call the day before."

"I can't face you on that day. I have a hard enough time facing myself."

"If she pulled the trigger, why do we keep punishing ourselves?" I shook my head. "And here I am dragging you back into the vault, the place where our ugly lies and deception flourish. You deserve better from your own son."

Dad sipped his coffee and then looked over at me. "Son, the

truth is, in many ways I've been trapped in the vault since the night she died. I knew this day would come, and I expected nothing less of you. There is no shame in confronting the truth. You understand how difficult it is to confront your failures; I have a lifetime of them. That night haunts me. Hits me the hardest when I'm alone. You might think I'm insensitive, but I know how to cry. Her death had to happen on your birthday. That is more than anyone deserves to endure. Why I did not have the common decency to avoid the entire incident only shows you a side of me that I will always regret."

I looked over at my father. "We both live in that fucking vault. At least we have that in common. But we also live on the surface." I smiled. "Remember when I would sit on your lap while you were writing, and watch the words appear on the blank piece of paper. And before long there was an entire page of words. And then we would go play catch before dinner. Those were the times I need to remember. That's what I think about on my birthday to get me through the day."

Dad reached over and took hold of my arm.

"I just don't want you to lose it like George did. I know you live a nightmare, about the night Margery died. George covered up his pain with hostility. You rebel. Do self-destructive things. I worry about what's lurking under all of that. You have the potential to really go way out there." My father stared at me. "I'm not the only one who's concerned about you."

I stared at Dad. "So Mark told you about the speech I made at the dump?"

Lee downed the rest of his coffee. "Of course he did. What kind of a brother do you think you have?"

"One that cares about me," I replied. "At times I escape to a safe world, one of my own creation. Dad, it's a place where we are always best friends and everything is perfect, just as I imagine it to be."

"Appreciate your imagination. Some people don't have any. Nothing wrong with playing out a fantasy, just don't get lost in your own mind. I don't want to find you crawling around in a swamp like George."

"If I ever end up like that, just remember a hug can go a long way. And while you're at it, give me a lift home."

"Agreed." Dad offered the bottom line. "That doesn't give you a hall pass to screw up again. You're responsible for your own actions. Be responsible!"

Out of respect I allowed my father to have the last word. I smiled like a Cheshire cat and flipped him off. Neither one of us had the ability to concede. That was our way, our mutual admiration. To seal our friendship, we shared a heartfelt hug with strong pats on the back.

***

No matter what I accomplished, this was the way my father saw me: it was never enough. As well it should be, for it was his job in life to keep pushing me up that mountain. Maybe one day he'll realize that standing on the same plateau was good enough.

Like the mythological phoenix, the relationship that my father and I shared arose from the ashes. A bond that had suffered from past circumstances was now restored. Our destinies once again united. Like the wondrous miracle of flight experienced by the rejuvenated phoenix, my father and I continued on our journey through life.

16

The Uris Heart

Arriving at Honolulu at two o'clock in the morning, a new flight crew came on board. We never left the plane, so Dad and I didn't have to clear customs. On this final leg of my journey we were the only two passengers.

I was a little jumpy. I still had to get my pot seeds through customs in Los Angeles, and the prospect of being thrown in jail amplified my anxiety level to near terror.

When the flight was about an hour away from Los Angeles, the captain informed Dad that he would just miss his connecting commercial flight to Denver. This did not sit well with my father, so following my suggestion, he insisted that the captain radio ahead and arrange that his outgoing flight be held until he arrived.

My father never failed to impress me when it came to dealing with airline executives and government officials. Not only did the commercial airlines hold the Denver flight for a half-hour, there were a couple of airline officials waiting to rush us through the airport, and quickly clear us through customs. Without wasting a second, customs agents hurried us through the checkpoint without opening a single piece of luggage.

Dad took my daypack from me as soon as we cleared customs, insisting that he needed it to hold the documents. He told me he planned on giving the FBI the documents inside the daypack in Denver as soon as he arrived. I had no choice except to hand it over. Lee promised to mail me the daypack as soon as he arrived in Colorado.

We hugged each other and I thanked Dad for the experience of a lifetime. He thanked me for not being too much of a pain in the ass during the trip. What wasn't said in those final moments of the trip, as we shared heartfelt smiles, meant more to us than any words.

A few days later, I received this letter from Lee:

Dear Son,

    Thank you for the most exciting research trip I can ever recall. To see you sweat it out all the way from Kabul to Los Angeles was worth the price of admission. You see Son, Andrei wasn't a Soviet General and the top-secret plans he sold me were bogus. Andrei is actually a distant relative of ours from Israel. He was in Kabul attending an agricultural conference on irrigation and crop rotation in arid climates. All of the documents you saw written in Russian were bogus and had nothing to do with invasion plans.

    Back in the States Bob Alterman and I devised the entire hoax over lunch one day, down to the smallest detail. For a final touch of realism to top off the charade, Andrei faked his own death and I took pills to make it appear as though I was sweating up a nervous storm.

    About the daypack and your marijuana seeds. For matters of safety while in Kabul I had Abdul drive you whenever you went out on your own. He informed me that you had contacted local smugglers. It took me a couple of days to figure out your scheme. So, while you were sleeping, I had Abdul's wife take out the hidden seeds in the daypack, then she carefully restitched the zipper lining so you wouldn't suspect anything was missing.

I'm not angry in the least that you failed at outsmarting me. I hope you learned your lesson and am somewhat ashamed of yourself. Better luck next time.

About the two girls in Kabul, that little side excursion to the prison, when Navid told us the girls were freed it was an incredible moment. To have their records expunged, and their lives no longer subject to scrutiny, although it will take a lifetime to recover from what they'd endured, at least they have that chance. And you helped. Never forget that.

As ever, your loving Dad

This was my reply:

Dear Dad,

I see, so it was all right for you to drive me crazy for the second half of our trip, worrying me to a near heart attack… that I would be shot for being a spy? Compared to my smuggling attempt, you should be apologizing to me!

Nevertheless, you certainly didn't fool me. Maybe it was the fact Andrei had the same name as your favorite fictional character from Mila 18. Maybe I noticed that Andrei wore a school ring from the University at Tel Aviv. What clinched my suspicion was the fact his Yiddish accent overly conflicted with his phony Russian accent. As a parting toast he ordered red wine instead of vodka. And finally, he wore hiking shorts and Israeli-made sandals with tall black socks, not exactly casual attire for a Kremlin General. And his faked death needed more realism as after his head slammed onto the table, apparently dead, I could see his breath fog up the glass on the top of the table.

As for the hundred seeds in the daypack you discovered back at the Kabul hotel. Have you ever heard of a decoy? You may have been paying for Abdul's services, but our devoted driver also took a bribe from me. The seeds his wife took out of the daypack were only wildflower seeds dipped in resin, looking like pot seeds to fool you. Remember how I fidgeted with the daypack lining, so you would take notice I was hiding something. And I had Abdul assist you in foiling my smuggling plan. I wanted you to think you'd outsmarted me. A few days before leaving Kabul I had Abdul's wife sew two hundred real indica seeds into the lining of my sports jacket. As a backup on that plan I placed another hundred seeds into the hollow handle of my movie camera, then sealed them from sight with black epoxy.

I never did it for the money. Like with you, it was all about the poker face. Besides the international intrigue gave us diversions that kept us from going out of our minds with boredom.

In Auckland, while you were taking a nap, I called Bob Alterman to arrange the final flights from New Zealand to Los Angeles. He contacted an old buddy of his who happened to be an executive working for the charter airlines. Bob also booked the final leg of your trip from Los Angeles to Denver on the commercial carrier. They delayed the final leg of the flight leaving Honolulu so you'd just barely miss your connecting flight to Denver. And I also counted on you radioing ahead to hold the Denver flight, and have airline officials waiting for us in Los Angeles to rush us through customs. It suited my smuggling plans.

It wasn't about the money. To prove it, enclosed is a cashier's check for 29,000 dollars. I took a grand out to fix my car. Give it to a needy charity.

I never for an instant believed Andrei was a Soviet defector. Come on Dad, you raised me to be smarter than that.

One more thing, what you did to free the two women in Kabul, and to insist it be kept discrete and anonymous, and even when Navid offered you gratitude, you acknowledged his efforts and not your own. In your letter you said I helped, but only in a small way. I helped you accomplish what few people have the heart, skill and persistence to do. I understand why you never took any credit, out of concern for the women, you stressed the importance of keeping their plight a private matter, and that is why I respect you all the more. You may say that it wasn't you who moved that mountain, but I was there and saw it with my own eyes.

Much love, Mike

And then, Lee:

Dear Son,

Thank you for the outstanding donation. It amazes me that you would risk your own freedom just to prove a point to me, although I am still trying to figure out exactly what the point was. I did forward your donation to an Israeli Hospital fund this morning, anonymously.

By the way, Andrei, or should I say our distant Israeli relative, and the Soviet documents were a decoy as well. Remember I recently wrote you that Bob was in on that hoax from its conception. Before Bob and I originally dreamed up the decoy hoax with Andrei, I was contacted in the States by the real Soviet defector who was in Afghanistan. The defector found out through my publisher that I would be in the country on a research trip conducting interviews, and he contacted me directly and agreed to give an interview, but it was not an interview he actually had in mind. He didn't ask for monetary compensation, he only wanted asylum for his entire family in the United States. I told Bob about the real defector. During a secret meeting in Kabul, the real defector gave me a grouping of microdots that contained extensive plans for the Soviet pre-invasion strategy and occupation of Afghanistan. I told the defector that I would bring his microdots with me to the States and then let our government decide if asylum was warranted. Knowing you would never use my electric shaver; I kept the dots hidden in my shaver's carrying bag. One of the airline officials at the Los Angeles airport who met us as our flight landed, and then rushed us through the airport customs... was actually my FBI contact. In Auckland I called Bob while you were out getting a haircut, after you booked the flights back to the States. Bob contacted the FBI for me and arranged for the drop off. I turned over the microdots to the FBI agent just after leaving the customs area on the way to my Denver flight.

Though in many respects you tried to outsmart me, always remember I got the last laugh. But I still owe you a good spanking for foolishly risking your freedom. For me this wasn't a trip around the world with a man and his son. It was a time I'll always treasure.

    As ever, your loving Dad

And my final letter:

Dear Dad,

    As you left customs at the Los Angeles airport to catch your Denver flight I saw you cleverly hand off the electric shaver's carrying bag containing the microdots. What you didn't realize, is the man who you thought was an FBI agent was in fact an up and coming character actor. He owed me a big favor for bribing an assistant district attorney to drop the charges, a few years back, when he got involved with a drug deal that went bad.

There was no real Soviet defector. The man who gave you the microdots in Afghanistan was a German salesman that Bob Alterman met years back. He was not a Soviet defector. He sold valves used in irrigation systems to Third World countries. Through correspondence Bob knew he would be in Afghanistan the same time as us, and that is when Bob initially contacted me and we thought up the entire scheme.

 I just got off the phone with Bob. Haven't laughed that hard in years. He's waiting for your call.

 Remember when I was six. Bob and you went off to lunch in town. And Bob's son and I washed his shiny new blue Thunderbird. It was by our own initiative, and we did it without want of reward. We did it because we desperately needed your praise. When you returned, boy were you both surprised. Chuck and I did the best job imaginable. This was the first car we'd ever washed, and searching for cleaning supplies we found stainless steel pads to apply the soapy water. And when we rinsed off the soapy water, there remained thousands of swirling scratches all over the car. Chuck and I were convinced of the spanking we'd get. But that wasn't the case at all. When Bob and you saw the car, instead of swift punishment, you broke out into uncontrollable sidesplitting laughter. Chuck and I knew that we were forgiven. So Dad, for all the mistakes I have made, thanks for realizing I'm a screw-up and laughing it off.

When I was little, I didn't want to monopolize your valuable time. I'd heard how important your work was, and that it helped others. And I'd sit on the lawn just outside your office, and watched my fingers dance in the grass. I listened to your keys as they struck the paper, I imagined you a master pianist headlining an orchestra. And I mimicked your every movement on the keyboard with my fingers on the grass. And this kept me occupied for hours. I waited patiently, and never knocked on the door. And even if you never came out of your office, it didn't matter to me at all, for I only wanted to be near you.

With love, Mike

A few days later, Lee's final letter:

Dear Son,

As soon as Bob contained himself, he finally confessed. He also said you went along with his scheme all in good fun, with no harm intended. I think we had the time of our lives interacting with Bob, that entertainment value alone outweighed all our efforts. About Hargrove reviving from his coma, if you orchestrated a hoax, I would be truly amazed, more so than if you actually sang the poor guy out of a coma. In that case fiction would be stranger than the truth.

Bob told me you were in on his hoax from the start, long before Bob and I initially devised the decoy hoax with Andrei. While I was busy setting up the Andrei hoax with our Israeli relative, Bob had plenty of time to finalize my meeting with the real 'phony' Soviet defector, the German salesman, and the handoff of the fake microdots. Bob also made all the arrangements with your actor buddy, to meet me at the Los Angeles airport. Bob knew an airline representative, who gained the actor access to the incoming flight and the customs area at the LA airport.

Bob said you phoned him from New Zealand to help arrange the final leg to Honolulu and Los Angeles on the medical charter flight. Although neither Bob nor you knew we would skip Tahiti, but you used it to your advantage.

And all the time I thought I was dealing with a real defector and real Soviet invasion plans for Afghanistan. Come to think of it, who in their right mind would ever believe the Soviet Union would waste their time invading an arid wasteland like Afghanistan?

Is it too much to hear that you're doing well scholastically? The best I can wish for is that you're happy. You should wish the same for your old man.

About Margery, the longer I avoided having that talk, the more ominous and unapproachable it became. I was afraid, not for what I did, or didn't do, to her. What terrified me would be to hear you say that we were through. And what I dreaded most in life never came to pass, for you chose the right words to say, and made the decision to keep me in your life.

You may not have realized it, but I knew when you were outside my office. I saw you at times through the window out of the corner of my eye. I witnessed your fingers typing in the grass. Your efforts were never in vain and I was moved that you wanted to be near me. On some of my longest days, when inspiration was nowhere to be found, and I couldn't type another word for whatever reason, I'd look outside and see you sitting with your fingers patiently posed above the grass, so how could I let you down.

With love, Dad

17

Falling From Grace

I came back from our trip with the greatest of expectations, feeling as though I could achieve anything. Of course, I still wanted to please Lee, more than ever. I had moved up in his estimation. Now, I was a first class adolescent rather than third class, but he still didn't see me as an adult. My long-term goal was to study filmmaking, but I needed some courses to fulfill the USC and Brooks admission requirements, so I started at Santa Monica College.

Inspired by Professor Kakar and Professor George, I took classes in sociology and anthropology. A few months later I dropped out. I tried my best, but a friend of mine had an apartment next to the campus and the nonstop flow of coeds and intoxicants took its toll on my already existing attention deficit disorder. Diversions or not, truth be told I just didn't have the attention span necessary to make it in college.

I began a career in the pornography business, writing and directing 8mm short films to be distributed by mail for personal use. I wrote under different pen names. We didn't use the word 'pornography' then. We called it adult educational material. The mother of a former schoolmate of mine dated a producer and distributor—we'll call him Dave—and I became his new sidekick with a head full of schemes and innovative ideas. All of my ventures reaped excessive rewards. So, in my own way, I entered the world of filmmaking and my exposure to the industry allowed me to hone my professional skills in a nonacademic atmosphere.

I told my mother that I worked for a seed catalog company; I don't think she was fooled. I told Lee the truth. He was not too pleased I dropped out of college, but he was happy to get the films I sent him.

When I returned from Afghanistan, Elaine, who had been dating a friend of mine in high school, reconnected with me in Santa Monica. I'd always liked her, and now that my buddy dumped her and moved to Hawaii, Elaine found pleasure in my company. So, we started to hang out on a regular basis.

Elaine was one of the three others I had introduced to *The Path of the Masters*, the book that had so influenced me. She and I had the same spiritual outlook and both followed a vegetarian diet. We loved nature and went for long hikes in the mountains and along the coastline, and trips out to the desert. She painted in watercolor and airbrushed in acrylics and I made exotic molded candles with driftwood. We vowed unconditional love to one another. Those promises soon faltered.

Elaine grew weary of my lowly career and thought it best for me to rise to a higher calling. At the time she worked as a nanny for the personal assistant to the world famous designer Charles Eames. The assistant pulled some strings and landed me a job as the design office's new field representative. I was really a no more than a glorified driver. It was a good time to leave the pornography business, because we'd recently been shut down by the Feds.

This was an incredible opportunity that any design student would treasure. Located in the mean streets of Venice, California, the office employed the most talented people I have ever known. I worked with each of them over the telephone as a field representative doing their research at universities and in public libraries, movie and sound studios, photographic laboratories, museums, and art supply stores. Sometimes, I had to locate rare objects. I also delivered the take-out food for the long sixteen-hour working days and cleaned the daily graffiti from the outside wall. When I wasn't driving around the city, they trained me to do more skilled jobs around the office like still and time-lapse photography. I loved my job.

While I worked there, we designed museum exhibits for the U.S. Bicentennial in Washington D.C. and traveling exhibits of historical figures like Isaac Newton, Copernicus and Galileo. Each exhibit contained graphic art, film clips and photographs, as well as live action interactive displays, along with detailed educational material presented through print and audio presentations.

At times, I would chauffer the mild mannered eccentric Charles around town. He was the type of guy who could solve age-old conundrums but was so mentally absorbed he forgot to tie his own shoelaces. In all the time I knew him he always wore the same plaid shirt and light brown corduroy pants and jacket. By no means were we close personal friends, but we spent mornings and afternoons together. I latched onto him as a gifted mentor and he enjoyed my company. He appreciated being liked for something other than his fame and professional expertise. Our times together were a delight.

I also dealt with Charles's wife Ray, who insisted on nothing less than perfection. With her hair tightly knotted in back, you would swear her brains were squeezed to the point of exploding. She looked like a chubby Victorian doll, always wearing a petticoat-lined brown dress, support stockings and smart shoes. One snap of her finger and I drove thirty miles to fetch her favorite ice cream. Then there was Ray's sweaty and smarmy office manager, an indentured relative, who was so tormented by Ray that his shoulders always sagged and his voice crackled with subservience. He became my nemesis, mainly because I wanted his job.

***

During that time, knowing our love would last forever, both Elaine and I at twenty, secretly married. The marriage was one of those pillow talk ideas, and two days later we were hitched at a nameless chapel in Riverside.

Within four months, Elaine left and moved to Hawaii. She felt trapped; neither one of us were ready for marriage. I remained in Los Angeles. I should have stayed in pornography; at least that kept her interested in me.

When Elaine walked out of my life it tore me up inside. I began another slide from reality, and I fueled the way with near lethal amounts of various narcotics. My work habits began to suffer. Even though I saw other women, the relationships were shallow compared to what I'd had with Elaine. The abandonment triggered something that had apparently been dormant, and grieving for Margery came back into the spotlight, at times it was far more of a cause for suffering than what was inspired by the loss of Elaine.

I tried to hold onto my job at the Eames Office, but soon found even that to be impossible and before long I was training my own replacement.

Nearing the end of my Eames career, while I was driving Charles back to his house after a lecture, I became weak from the drugs in my system and nearly crashed the car into a willow tree, mere yards away from his house. We walked the rest of the way and he invited me to come in and rest before heading out. I entered his home and stretched out on a couch.

***

Trapped in a surrealistic dream world due to the excessive narcotics flowing through my veins, everything that happened over the following period of time seemed abstract and disjointed.

That afternoon at Charles' home while I rested on the couch, he made a couple of phone calls. A few minutes later he suggested a course of action that might be just what I needed. Charles talked me into going to live with a woman named Carla. She was recently widowed and lonely and needed someone to keep her company. She was busy during the week, but she needed someone to spend time with on long Sunday afternoons.

Considering my current mental instability and excessive drug use, Charles thought this would be a perfect opportunity to take some time off away from the pressures of everyday life. Since I had nothing to lose and everything to gain, I agreed to meet with Carla and see if we were compatible. Someone arrived to drive me to her home. Exhausted, I took a nap along the way.

Carla's stylish old world mansion was in a rural part of Brentwood. She stood at the front door and waved hello. Somewhere nearing forty, and very attractive with short dirty blond hair, and wearing professional businesswomen's attire, Carla welcomed me into her home. She worked at her younger brother's office in a nearby town, some kind of international trade consulting business.

After entering her lavishly decorated home, Carla and I walked upstairs to a room with hardwood floors and giant picture windows that overlooked the courtyard of her palatial estate. I couldn't keep my eyes open and I fell asleep.

***

Much to my surprise, when I opened my eyes the next morning, Carla was there to greet me. She invited me to go with her on a long drive, to a racetrack just across the border in Mexico. Although still foggy, I gladly agreed to go with her.

What a welcomed turn of fate. One minute I was near overdosing on drugs and losing my grasp on reality, and the next minute I found myself sitting in the comfortable black leather passenger seat of a shiny new Lincoln Continental, next to a beautiful, classy woman. She drove for a couple of hours as we ate snacks and drank sodas. We bonded instantly over the loss of a spouse. She was a widow and I understood that her loss was greater than mine with Elaine.

We finally arrived at the racetrack in Caliente, just south of the Mexican border. Carla liked to place heavy bets on the trifecta horse races, and this would turn out to be her lucky day. After only an hour at the racetrack we headed back with nearly a hundred thousand dollars in undeclared cash.

The Lincoln contained hidden compartments; hiding places in which the Border Customs Inspectors would never find the winnings from the racetrack. After clearing the border with ease we continued on our journey home.

Carla invited me to stay at her Brentwood estate for as long as I wanted. With only a bachelor apartment to go back to, I gratefully accepted her offer. Wanting nothing in return for the free rent and board, Carla only wished me to get back on my feet and she suggested I start my own small business to pass the time.

Her friendship alone was more than enough to keep me from falling back into drug addiction. She understood I wanted to change my life, she helped me devise the perfect plan to get back on my feet.

The plan wasn't exactly legal, but as long as every move was calculated to perfection, she thought it worth the risk. Money was never an issue to me. I always had what I needed. I wanted to be involved in this new venture because Carla inspired me and she felt it would improve my self-esteem.

The next morning, I set the plan into action. With Carla's financial backing, I purchased a shiny, new, yellow taxicab with two wide green leather seats. I built in a few undetectable hidden compartments which could conceal nearly a hundred-fifty pounds of contraband.

I had a connection in Mexico, Gomez, who lived just south of the border. He sold jars of pharmaceutical grade pills for next to nothing. Gomez was the guardian of the town and surrounding area and desperately needed weapons to arm the locals so they could defend themselves against the drug lords.

I knew a man named Jake 'the Snake' who had been a lieutenant in Vietnam. Now, he was a survivalist who owned many automatic guns, but needed lots of cocaine, both for his personal use and for his various connections.

I also knew a chemist named Samson, who ran a drug laboratory that manufactured and distributed pharmaceutical cocaine, but he wanted to branch out into the more profitable distribution of designer drugs like LSD and Mescaline.

And then there was Miles. He was a chemist known in the

underworld for manufacturing the finest designer drugs, but he wanted pharmaceutical grade pills.

Except for Gomez, all of my connections were within a few miles of Carla's estate.

I secured legal papers from a handicapped filing clerk named Esmeralda who worked in the basement of the Department of Motor Vehicles. I think she had some kind of crush on me as she helped me out of a few traffic tickets in the past, and now willingly forged a valid taxi operator's license, and legal registration, plus new license plates. All of this was necessary so I could operate the taxi in both California and Mexico.

Carla had a friend come by the house to trim my hair and give me new inconspicuous clothing to wear. In my sports coat and a button-down shirt, I now resembled a scholar like my brother—I even wore a tie.

***

Early Sunday morning, I got into my yellow taxicab and headed over to Jake's where I bought a carload of automatic weapons and ammunition. Then Jake and I hid the weapons in the secret compartments of my modified taxi.

From Jake's place, I drove to a retirement complex just next door to Carla's house. Representing a charitable foundation, I had previously posted an offer on their bulletin board for all expenses paid Sunday trips into Mexico. It just so happened that three senior citizens signed up. They loved to get out in the world every chance they could, so I filled up the taxi with three energetic senior citizens and we headed down the coast.

My highly talkative passengers were very sweet and very old. Bill, who sat next to me in the front seat, lent his talents as a navigator and constantly kept me informed of the roadway up ahead. The two women sitting in the back were named Debra and Cynthia and they kept me engaged in interesting conversation most of the time. Upon arriving in Mexico we did a little sightseeing and shopping. Then, I treated them to a complimentary lunch.

My friend Gomez owned a warehouse that was next door to the restaurant. While my three passengers ate their lunch, Gomez and I unloaded the weapons from the taxi and filled the hidden compartments with several jars of pharmaceutical grade pills. After lunch, I drove my passengers back through the border crossing undetected.

We headed north for a couple of hours and kept ourselves entertained, chatting all the way. The last thing I wanted to do was rush. The seniors listened to my adolescent stories and never judged me for making the wrong decisions in life. Then, they shared their experiences with me, showing me that I was not the only person in the world who made bad decisions. When we arrived back in Brentwood, I dropped my passengers off at the old age home.

I would drive the taxi to where my chemist friend Miles lived. We took the pills out of the hidden compartments and loaded up the taxi with sealed jars of designer drugs. From there I drove to Samson's and traded designer drugs for pharmaceutical cocaine, then went to Jake's and traded cocaine for more automatic weapons.

Then, I drove back to the Brentwood house, just in time for Carla and I to go for a drive around her neighborhood in her Lincoln Continental. We parked and watched the sunset, and ate ice cream. After that we returned home. I was exhausted from the long Sunday, so I went straight to my room and fell asleep.

Every Sunday from then on, I drove the taxi across the Mexican border, traveling with the same three people from the retirement home. At times I nearly forgot all about the guns and drugs. Eventually, I looked forward to Sunday—just so I could spend time with all of my new friends.

During the week I occupied my hours reading philosophy in my room. Only once in a while did I venture out to sit in the backyard sunlight or go visit with Esmeralda in her basement office at the Department of Motor Vehicles. Carla was usually at work till late or out of town during the week so I only spent time with her on Sunday afternoons.

My smuggling business kept me occupied every Sunday for twenty weeks. My cut for the drug and weapon trades, earned me around ten thousand dollars profit for each transaction. That money was kept in a safe in Carla's office. Each Sunday netted close to fifty grand.

Carla would be anxiously waiting for me when I got back every Sunday afternoon. Usually, we stopped for ice cream and watched the sunset. Even though she was beautiful, I never once made a pass at her. Somehow I just did not think of her in that way.

My friendships with Carla, Bill, Cynthia and Debra grew stronger and everything in my life seemed to be so much simpler. My new friends had faith in me, and that made all the difference.

One Sunday afternoon Carla and I were relaxed as ever, sitting in her car, parked on a cliff overlooking an incredible panoramic view of the sun setting into the ocean. I kept my eyes focused on the beautiful colors in the sky. "I've lost the desire to continue."

"Continue with...?" she asked.

"I don't want to go on with the gunrunning and the drug smuggling. I just forgot what the point of the plan was? I never did it for the money. What am I doing this for?"

Carla reached out and took hold of my arm. "I don't want you to be confused. I want you to come back."

"Back from where?"

"Trust me, Michael. You are almost there."

I closed my eyes and relaxed. "Carla, I don't know what's going on anymore."

"Michael, where are we?"

I opened my eyes and looked around. "Sitting in your car. Why?"

"What do you see?"

My frustration surfaced. "Shit Carla, the damn sun just went down! Colors in the sky. The ocean. Waves. The beach. The hood of your car, the street behind us in the rearview mirror? What am I missing?"

"Please don't get upset. It's not like you." Carla closed her eyes.

I leaned over and kissed her cheek. "I want to get there. I want to come back to where I used to be. Problem is: I've been lost for so long."

"You have to make up your own mind and decide what is best. I am only here to help."

With firm resolve I declared, "Next Sunday, I want to take all the money I made over the last few months down to Mexico. I want you to bet it all on a trifecta. We can give the money to charity."

"That is a sound plan." Reaching up she gently ran her fingers through my hair. "I'd like to come along, very much so. And if you don't mind I'd like to bring along a friend of mine. Her name is Grace," said Carla. "I told her about you, and she is looking forward to spending some time with you."

Early the next Sunday morning I found myself sitting in the front seat of the yellow taxi. It was almost as though I'd spent the entire night there and didn't want to miss the ride. Just seconds later everyone else arrived and cheerfully got into my taxi. Carla put a large suitcase in the trunk, probably holding all the money for the bet.

Carla sat between Bill and me in the front seat. Carla's guest for the day sat in the backseat, in the middle between Cynthia and Debra. She wore a hat with a veil covering her face.

"My name is Grace," she said.

"Hello," I replied. Her voice sounded familiar.

We headed out and eventually crossed the border into Mexico.

It was a great day at the Caliente racetrack. Grace continued to wear the veil over her face. Carla picked all three winners on the trifecta. We had small fortune in currency, and were unable to fit it all into the hidden compartments, and it overflowed into the cab and the trunk. We then headed back towards the border and waited our turn to clear the customs checkpoint.

Upon arriving at the checkpoint the guard looked over my papers and motioned for me to wait for a more comprehensive inspection. This had never happened before, not once during the past twenty weeks. A couple of armed border guards approached with drug sniffing dogs, and the dogs immediately began to bark. They had found one of my secret compartments, one that I had forgotten about, with a few pounds of cocaine inside that had been sitting there for the past week.

Threatened with incarceration, I found it increasingly hard to breathe, and realized this would be my only chance to make a break. So I asked, "Bill, what should I do?"

Bill did not hesitate. "We have to make a run for it!"

All the women nodded.

I floored the accelerator and the taxi bolted away from the armed Customs Inspectors. Everyone in the car was terrified and held on tight. The Customs Inspectors immediately drew their weapons and aimed and fired a slew of shots at the taxi, busting out the back window, and filling the car with scattered bullets. I kept racing forward swerving around traffic. We eventually made it to the open highway. We were going so fast it was as if the other cars were standing still.

When we were in the clear, we pulled off the highway and into a recreational area with trees and a lake. It was crowded with people picnicking. I parked the taxi.

Grace leaned forward and gently whispered in my ear, "Michael, I've been shot."

Bill, Carla, Cynthia and Debra got out of the taxi and just stood there. Rushing to the back, I carefully laid Grace down on the seat. I sat down and placed her head on my lap and gently touched the veil that covered her face.

Grace gently squeezed my hand. "Michael."

I finally recognized her voice. "Margery?"

I slowly lifted her veil.

"Michael... I'm dying."

How was I going to deal with this situation? Everything seemed so strange. This woman lying before me with her head on my lap was someone I loved dearly. How could this possibly be? Margery died in my arms in Colorado, and now it was happening again.

I held her body and felt her warm breath upon my face. I smelled her unique fragrance, one like no other. As she gazed into my eyes, I captured rivers of love flowing from her heart. My feelings for her were the same—a love so real I could perceive it with all my senses.

"I'm sorry, Margery. For letting you die that night in Colorado," I said in a whisper.

"There was never any blame, so don't blame yourself. You tried but failed to save me then, and you can't save me now."

"I should be in your place."

"That night your destiny was to survive, and now it is to live. You did everything to make me feel loved and wanted, what more could anyone give."

It was then I realized why I was reliving this same experience over again. All of this seemed to be nothing more than a strange dream. Somehow she'd found her way back to me, if only to rescue me from my own unrelenting guilt and crippling sorrow. Trapped emotions surged from within, and I began to cry.

I asked, "Is any of this real?"

"What we once had is real." She sighed. "What remains, you have to let go of."

"Let me see your smile. It is how I need to remember you this time."

With a loving smile she whispered, "I'm happy whenever you are near." Then, Margery closed her eyes and became motionless.

I would remember that smile for the rest of my life. She reminded me of a fallen angel, so radiant and pure. The only thing left for me to do was to rock her lifeless body in my arms and allow the pain of her passing to wash over me. A powerful presence had been trapped in my subconscious for so many years. I now allowed it to come to the surface and dissipate. I cried for several minutes.

***

Carla walked over to my side, and reached out and took hold of my arm. "It is time to let her go, Michael."

I continued to look at Margery's sweet smile. "I wish I could." I didn't want to let her go, but I had to, that is what Margery wanted. So I closed my eyes and let her go.

When I opened my eyes, as if by magic, Margery was gone.

I was sitting in the back seat of the taxi all alone.

Still crying, I turned to Carla. "Margery disappeared. What's going on? None of this seems real. Please, help me."

Bill and Cynthia and Debra all came over to join Carla beside the car. They gently pulled me from the taxi. I stood and looked around. It was at that very instant everything changed right before my very eyes. I was no longer standing next to a taxi, and there was not a recreational area filled with people, and there were no trees, and no lake, and no cars.

I was in a yellow room. The green taxi seats had become two green couches. And Bill, Cynthia and Debra were not senior citizens; they couldn't have been more than fifty years old. Nothing about Carla had changed.

I asked, "What's going on? What am I doing in this yellow room?"

With a smile Carla confirmed, "Welcome back, Michael. We have been waiting for you. Just be calm, everything is going to be all right." She touched my forehead and suggested, "Go to sleep."

***

When I woke up, I was sitting on a black leather reclining chair. The first thing I noticed was a painting of an ice cream shop with people eating ice cream cones. On another wall was a photograph of the Caliente racetrack. On another wall of her office hung a large oil painting of a glorious sunset. Slowly, the pieces of the puzzle began to fit into place.

Before long a familiar face entered the room. Carla approached me and sat down in a second black leather chair right next to mine. She asked, "Are you sitting in an automobile?"

Puzzled, I answered, "No... I'm sitting in a chair."

"Good." She reached over and took a folder out and began to write notes on a piece of paper. Keeping focused on the page, she asked, "Do you remember what just happened to you?"

"Margery died in the backseat of a yellow taxi. No, she died on a green couch in a yellow room. No, she died in Colorado years ago." I leaned back. "I'm having a hard time distinguishing between what was real and what I imagined."

"Relax. You still need some time to come back—all the way."

"Back from where?"

"A while back you suffered a complete mental breakdown. The drugs in your system created a chemical imbalance in your brain that led to initiating your mind's escape into a schizophrenic world. You have been trapped in your subconscious, in a world of your own making."

"How long have I been out of it?"

Carla kept writing down notes. "How long do you think you've been out of it?"

I thought for a few moments. "I made twenty runs down to Mexico on every Sunday, plus today." I confirmed, "About twenty-one weeks."

"Actually, Michael, you have only been here for twenty-five days. You relived Sunday after Sunday. There were no other days of the week."

"I am more confused than ever."

"What is the last thing you remember before you were brought here?"

"I remember driving Charles back from a lecture. I was on a lot of drugs. I rested on his couch while he made a couple of phone calls. Charles told me about you, and then someone drove me here, to this house."

Carla pointed at a large photograph of the racetrack on the wall. She then pointed at the reclining black leather chair. "We never left this office during our Sunday afternoon drives." She then pointed at the large painting of a sunset and of the ice cream parlor. "Our afternoon drives through the neighborhood, watching the sunsets, eating ice cream... none of it was real."

"But my books...? I read philosophy books all the time during the evenings and during the week, for hundreds of hours."

"You never had any books. You only recalled what you had previously read. When you were in your room you either slept or sat in a chair and just stared at a blank wall. You were practically catatonic. All your meals were handfed to you. Remember, you have only been here for twenty-five days."

I asked, "I never left this Brentwood estate, not even once?"

"We are in the countryside, four hours north of London," Carla said.

"England!"

"You were between an imaginary world and borderline catatonic. We used assorted cocktails of psychotherapeutic drugs, radical ones not allowed in the States. Once the drugs were introduced into your system we started the main part of the treatment."

"Drugs. That explains the dizziness and tunnel vision."

Carla studied my eyes for a few moments. "It should wear off after a bit." She continued to write down notes. "Would you like anything, water, a snack?"

I joked, "No thanks, I'm still stuffed from being handfed." Sitting back in the chair, I watched as she continued to write. "How could you fathom what was going on in my mind?"

"You never fought us as we ventured deeper into your mind, into your subconscious. We stuck to a specific plan and paid close attention to every detail."

I asked, "You said we?"

"We, as in 'the team.' Sometimes we used mere suggestion and other times reverted to deep layers of hypnosis and slowly, in just over twenty-one days, we brought you deeper and deeper into a fabricated world, until we reached the source of your most significant trauma. While you thought we were driving down to Mexico and around town in a Lincoln Continental, you were under hypnosis. We were able to learn a great deal about your past and what was crippling you. With that information the team controlled every aspect of your treatment here, although we carefully allowed you to think you were in total control, we had orchestrated everything. Then, once the psychotherapy drugs took hold, and we totally gained your trust, we confronted you with the most traumatic event from your past, using mere substitutions of people, places and events, in hopes to snap you out of our schizophrenic prison. In the beginning, through hypnosis, I learned more about your breakup with Elaine, but that was only the surface. Digging deeper, our team soon understood, that your stepmother, Margery, was the source of your real trauma, and how her death significantly affected the past six years of your life. Grace was never real, and the Margery you watched die in the taxi was only a suggestion the team implanted in your mind."

"You keep saying—'the team'?"

"Everyone you have seen since you arrived here last month is part of the team, five of us are trained professionals, and others just wanted to help. We gave the team names that represented influential people from your past." Carla stood up and reached out her hand. "Come. Everyone is waiting to now meet the real you for the first time."

I took her hand and stood up. Then I asked, "Am I still crazy?"

"Don't worry. I think you'll be all right." Carla gave me a hug. Holding my hand, she started to walk down the hallway of her mansion. "You do understand that I am a psychiatrist?"

"And all this time I thought you were just my friend. Thank you."

She winked, "You're welcome. And yes, I am your friend."

***

We walked out of her office and ventured downstairs till we reached the large yellow painted room that overlooked the street. The two green couches sat, one behind the other, just as the two rows of seats in the taxi. Watching me as I entered, everyone I'd remembered from the past twenty-five days sat around the room. Going from person to person, I hugged them and shook their hands and thanked them for helping me. Even though I learned all their real names, I still used the fictional names that I was more comfortable with.

Samson and Miles were architects who lived next door. Jake was a psychiatrist who worked out of Carla's clinic in town; his automatic weapons were a few assorted hundred-year-old antique pistols and rifles from his collection. Gomez was an actor who did theater work in London and was in town visiting his family, his Mexican warehouse was the toolshed in the courtyard. A British housekeeper and cook who came by every day, Esmeralda, played the role of the DMV clerk, her office was the basement where she did the laundry. All of the pills and drugs and cocaine were items like beans and flour and sugar from her pantry. And the restaurant in Mexico was the dining room.

Bill, Cynthia and Debra were well-respected therapists who lived nearby.

Everyone involved maintained confidentiality, and having known Carla for several years all of them donated their time. As for Carla's role in all of this, it remained a mystery. I never did get a straight answer out of her, of how she was contacted and by whom, let alone who paid for my flight to England and all the therapy drugs. Her best response was a wink.

We sat down to dinner. Now that they were all together, I thanked everyone collectively. I would have never guessed my life was heading so far away from reality, not unlike George's experience after burying his wife at sea. Without the team's help, one can only wonder where I might have ended up. This was the last time I remembered seeing any of them. Emotionally exhausted, right at the dinner table, I closed my eyes, lowered my head and took a nap.

***

The next thing I could remember was regaining consciousness while sitting on a bench in the middle of a sunlit garden. I was back in California in a familiar setting. A man wearing a plaid shirt and a corduroy jacket was sitting next to me on the bench. It was a warm pleasant day and all the flowers were in full bloom. The man smiled at me, then leaned back and allowed the sunlight to warm his face. I closed my eyes and turned my face towards the sun.

"Good, you finally woke up," Charles said.

"Funny," I said. "A minute ago I was sitting at a dining room table with..." I shrugged my shoulders and felt the warm sun on my face. "I think I've been out of town for the past month."

"And what did you accomplish?" Charles asked.

"I'm not certain. Maybe, maybe it doesn't matter where I was or what I did." I glanced over at Charles. "It's good to be here."

"It certainly is a beautiful day." Charles looked at me and smiled.

"If something was important, you'd tell me, right?"

"Best to let some things go." Charles placed his hand on my shoulder. "What you do now is important."

I thought for a few moments. "I've been thinking about a camera repair school in Denver. I'll be close to my father and brother. That's important."

"That reminds me." Charles reached into his coat pocket, took out a letter-sized envelope and handed it to me. "It's from a friend."

My name was on the outside of the envelope. Inside was a photograph. I had no recollection of where and when the photo was taken. I sat in the front left. My eyes were closed. There was Carla, Samson, Jake, Miles, Esmeralda, and all the team in England. And yet, Margery was there, too, in the bottom right. How odd I thought to myself as I placed the picture back into the envelope. I always loved a good mystery, and it would be some time before I realized the truth about the photo. But that is another story in itself.

"So this is goodbye." I smiled at Charles.

"Take care of yourself."

"I'll never forget your help."

"No mention." He smiled. "My driver will be here soon."

I asked, "Can I hitch a ride into town?"

"Your ride has already been arranged."

I wondered, "Another mystery?"

"Let me help." Charles looked at me. "The solution to every mystery lies in its origin. Go back in time, back to where it all began. Our lives continually project forward. Where you were then is a past reflection of where you are now. What is your first significant memory?"

"I told you that memory a while back." I closed my eyes and relaxed. "I'm sitting on the lawn outside my father's office. I'm typing on an imaginary typewriter, my fingers dancing on the surface of the grass in unison with the sound of typing coming from inside his office. This orchestral interplay seemed to go on for hours. Then all of a sudden the sound of typing stops, and I also stop typing. Moments later my father emerges from his office. He smiles at me, takes hold of my hand and helps me to my feet. I turn and see my brother standing on the edge of the lawn. Throughout my life, as did my father, Mark Jay watched my every move, protecting me from afar, and patiently waited for me to join him. That afternoon my brother held a football, and my father and I joined him for a game of catch before dinner."

Charles said, "There never was any mystery."

I patted him on the shoulder. "Apparently not."

"They asked if you were happy." Charles shrugged his shoulders, faced the sun and closed his eyes.

"Yes, I am."

"Tell them yourself." He pointed towards the driveway.

I stood up and walked down the driveway to where a large black sedan with tinted windows was waiting. My father got out of the back door. Out of the other side emerged my brother. Both of them smiled and greeted me with open arms. For me, this had always been, and will always be, the real Uris Trinity.

***

Like my father before me, I learned to survive the darkest caverns within my own personal vault. Time and time again, to make me a better person, Dad pushed me off the edge of the cliff towards oblivion. That was his way. Ironically, he never stopped loving me, and was always there to rescue me from the fall. He had always been my most challenging ally and greatest adversary. Neither one of us surrendered, nor claimed victory over the other. A father and son could share no greater love, or higher respect. With fact and fiction, he strengthened my character and cared about me in ways that I am just beginning to fully appreciate. His wish was that I embrace my imagination. For what is within, you will never be without.

Epilogue 1973 - 2016

Dad was there for me throughout my life, although at times I hardly noticed. I thought his love had too many conditions, yet looking back that criticism was formulated when I was a child. My father sacrificed everything for love. I will always honor him and treasure his wisdom.

Dad bettered our world, at times sacrificing his happiness in the process. It was inevitable a toll had to be taken. When his third marriage failed, he ran away, isolating himself off the coast of New York, on an island retreat near Hemingway's Sag Harbor. It pained him greatly to be displaced from my younger half brother and sister, Conor and Rachael. Living on Shelter Island, he met a lovely woman named Channing. They created a wonderful children's book that she illustrated. It has yet to be published.

Even with his fondest intentions, their union faltered. Once again Lee lost against the ravages of time in thinking he could sustain a long-term relationship. He could never separate the anger that his father had instilled in him from his loving, affectionate self. Sadly, his last chance at a meaningful relationship departed the island on an afternoon ferry. He spent his final years trying to reconstruct relationships that could never be repaired. Most of his good friends, like Bob, had passed away. Although he craved affection, his remaining loved ones distanced themselves. Only a reflection of the man standing before the mirror remained.

I followed in my father's footsteps and managed to rack up three failed marriages. Dad understood me. This apple had not fallen far from the tree. In our hearts, we were great men. But even that greatness could not free us from the vaults of our past. The stepchildren I raised, Terryn, Tyler, Thomas and Andy, although we live far apart, have always been the light in my life. Each new generation triumphs over mistakes of the past. Thanks to evolution, my children are instilled with the wisdom they need to survive.

Like my father before me, I seek refuge away from my dark side. I stopped running. I have settled on the Monterey Peninsula, with an inspiring view of the Pacific from my windows. Lee's favorite author, John Steinbeck, lived here, and I understand why. I write in solitude. It's better that way. My world now is a panoramic view and a walk along the shoreline. Destiny placed me in one of the most beautiful places on earth, from where I continue to reflect and grow.

My brother and I never deserted our father, as so many other people did. Mark Jay and I always picked up the phone when it rang. As Dad grew older, our visits with him became more frequent. Lee wanted me to come live with him on the island. Saying no was the hardest decision of my life. It was best we treasured our relationship as it stood—any number of our unresolved issues from the past were bound to resurface and undermine anything good we shared. In that light, I was no different than he. For instance, I never fully believed that Lee and I had buried the hatchet concerning Margery. If he had pushed me into a corner, I would have used the same cruel words he had used on her.

I was born the year my father published his first novel, and I knew him his entire published career. We had our moments—of pride fused with anger, and of hope blended with sorrow. Our life was a new adventure every day. As my father's health declined, he became a prisoner within his home. Where we sat on his wooden deck overlooking Chase Creek, we would talk for hours. We solved the riddles of the universe. Until the very end, he insisted I call his travel agent and book two tickets to Jerusalem as he was convinced he had a way to finally bring lasting peace to the Middle East. Such determination was the mark of a man who never lost faith in his people. We never made that journey. Maybe we should have. Some things are never meant to be.

In 2003, at his home on Shelter Island, my father left the last few words of his final novel unwritten. Inspiration for all of humanity, we had lost a man who never stopped his search for the meaning in life. His words of wisdom will echo for thousands of years. Few treasured the wealth of love and compassion as Dad did. To lose his dignity and decay in a hospital bed had never been my father's way. In the end, it was his choice to pass. To die with grace in his home was a right he deserved.

Almost two years to the day my father passed away, my mother joined him in the afterlife. Betty had always been the stability in my life, a safe anchor in stormy seas. She spent the remainder of her days with my stepfather Frank, a kind and loving man. In their relationship, a harsh word was never spoken. My father was the love of her life and she deserved the best in life, but living with my father came with too many compromises. As for my sister, our relationship flourishes to this day. Karen always taught me to look towards the light, and in my darkest hours her words meant the world to me. We often have different perspectives on life, as most siblings do. We are strong-willed individuals, but we care about one another as every brother and sister should. Respect and love are attributes we both hold dear—lessons that our parents instilled in us.

It has been forty-five years since Margery passed. Only kind thoughts of her loving nature remain. Every year on my birthday, I go to my storage locker and retrieve a large crate. I open it in my private room, an inner vault where it takes all of my courage to enter. Inside the crate is a portrait of a woman that I will always love. Wherever her soul is, I pray that she joins me on this day. Holding the frame, my hands tremble as I gaze into her painted eyes. My beautiful friend— during these moments I treasure her love. This is my glimpse into a surrealistic world of beauty and splendor, where my imagination soars and our souls merge together. At last, we are free. Tears confirm my undying feelings for her. Surviving her has been a life sentence of remorse. I cannot change what happened. My heart remains fated to relive her death, every year on my birthday. And when my conscience has finished with me, I emerge from my vault and return the portrait to its resting place. It will be another year till we visit again.

My father spent a lifetime distancing himself from his father whereas my brother and I cherished our father. We were the proud creations of a master storyteller. Our finer attributes are reflections of a great humanitarian. In trying to please our father, my brother and I chose entirely different paths, and even though at times we were at odds with him, we never lost respect for the real Leon Uris—the patient and caring, ordinary dad.

Observing my brother and following his lead, I realized I had to become my own person. I could never dream of equaling Lee's accomplishments. His voice touched the hearts of millions of admirers, and all that I am is one of them. Dad became his own mountain. I am grateful that he overshadows me. I was lucky to have a brother who was there for me. Throughout life Dad and Mark Jay held my hand crossing every street, reminding me to look both ways, protecting me from harm. They are with me now as I type, inspiring every word.

Mark Jay, the heir apparent, became the family patriarch. Where my father aspired to greatness, my brother never had to try for, in my eye, he was born the perfect person. Loved and respected by almost everyone he met, he selflessly enriched the lives of others. His unceasing humor, warmth and charm lifted the spirits of everyone who met him. I had hoped to spend our declining years together, my best friend and I. We would sit on some front porch somewhere, and with nothing better to do, we would watch the sunset. That is all I wanted out of life.

Three years after my father passed on, I found myself standing in a hospital room. Next to me were my brother's wife Patricia and their two daughters, Shannon and Brittany. Recollections of last time I looked at him, face to face, play on in an endless loop in my mind. His eyes seemed to be calling out to me, for what reason I'll never know. The heartbreak that I could not save him haunts me. But it had not been my decision alone, and the four of us stood helplessly and watched the nurse disconnect the IV solutions and machines that had kept our loved one alive. And our hearts shattered. The most important part of our lives had gone. We outlived my brother, and in his passing, our fondest aspirations were crushed. Like my father, my brother was a great man. Mark Jay taught us to carry on, even if he could not join us. In that, he left us no choice but to honor his wish.

I see my brother's searching eyes wherever I go, it is all that I have left of him, and even though it destroys me to remember that day, it reminds me of how precious life is, and how important love is to us all. I had always been the reckless one who defied death on a daily basis.

Mark Jay stood for everything good in life. Why he departed before me makes no sense at all. I miss my brother. Each new day is only another without him. If I ever come to terms with my grief, it will be on a front porch, somewhere along the way. I will watch the sunset alone, and I will try my best to smile because he would have wanted it that way. For I know it is far better to bear the pain of losing him than to lose what memory of him remains.

***

In later life, my father had to ascend four flights of stairs to reach his bedroom. Due to his fading health, each step was a challenge. And the very last flight of stairs became the hardest. He had to stop and rest on the way up. And I stood below and watched as he leaned against the wide banister, just as he had leaned against a podium while giving a speech. This is how I best remember my father. This was his crowning achievement, looking out at his adoring public. A thousand faces in the crowd hung on his every word, as he transported his audience from the depths of despair to the heights of inspiration. It is indeed an art to move the coldest hearts and have an entire auditorium shed tears. The level of pride I felt in those moments never faded.

I am humbled and proud to be his son. When it came down to it he didn't care about fame or glory, for all he ever wanted out of life was to love and be loved. This is why I wrote this book. I wanted to share my feelings about an extraordinary man, one with a tremendous heart. And when the speech was finished, my father turned to me and smiled, and before heading to his final destination, he raised his hand and waved good-bye.

Photo Captions & Credits

All photos are from the Uris Family Archives, unless otherwise stated.

Front Cover:
Lee, Margery, Michael
Photo of Lee: Jill Uris
Photo of Margery and Michael: Uris Family Archives

Preface:
Michael, Lee, Mark

Introduction:
Page 1: Gang and Michael (right) at Hesby Street home, Encino, California

Chapter 1. Exodus:
Page 3: Lee, Mark, Karen, Betty and Michael in Palm Springs
Page 4: Betty and Michael at Hesby Street home
Page 7: Lee and Betty 1944, stationed in San Francisco
Page 9: Lee with David Ben Gurion in Israel
Page 11: Michael, Karen, Mark in Rome
Page 19: Lee writing *Exodus* at Hesby Street home office

Chapter 2. Fuckin' French Assassin:
Page 21: Mark and Michael | Lee in Israel

Chapter 3. The Triangle:
Page 35: Margery Edwards
Page 36: Clipping from Los Angeles Times, 1966

Acknowledgements

A special thanks to Stephanie Workman, for her gifted expertise and faith in my words. I would also like to thank Victoria Parker Jones, Laurie Horowitz, Terryn Grace and Harper Elizabeth Hendrickson, Tyler Henry Tangalin, Dave Schoonover, Willemien van der Walt and Jeffrey Workman.

About the Author

Michael currently lives on the Monterey Peninsula, the same natural setting that inspired John Steinbeck. Having had a lifelong working association with his novelist father Leon Uris, Michael grew up in a literary atmosphere some may consider privileged. As with everything in life, he experienced equal shares of happiness and heartbreak, honor and disgrace. Michael assisted his father with interviews and research, and this facilitated the evolution of his own writing process. A philosopher and naturalist at heart, Michael spends his days writing in a studio that overlooks the rugged California coastline.

Read Michael's blog at: www.michaelcadyuris.com
Follow Michael on Facebook: fb.me/TheUrisTrinity

Manufactured by Amazon.ca
Bolton, ON

31455426R00169